STUDIES IN ENGLISH LITERATURE

Volume XCII

AN "IDLE SINGER" AND HIS AUDIENCE

A Study of William Morris's
Poetic Reputation in England, 1858–1900

by

DELBERT R. GARDNER

1975
MOUTON
THE HAGUE - PARIS

© Copyright 1975
Mouton & Co. B.V., Publishers, The Hague

No part of this book may be translated or reproduced in any form by print, photoprint, microfilm, or any other means, without written permission from the publishers.

ISBN 90 279 3383 9

Printed in The Netherlands

PREFACE

William Morris's first volume of poetry, *The Defence of Guenevere, and other Poems* (1858), made little impression on either public or critics, and what attention it did receive was largely unfavorable. Full recognition of the poet's ability was delayed almost a decade, but the enthusiastic reception of *The Life and Death of Jason* (1867) and the even greater acclaim accorded *The Earthly Paradise* (1868-70) catapulted Morris into lasting fame; for the rest of his life, he remained a figure of national—and international—prominence. By 1877, his fame as a poet was great enough to secure him an invitation to stand for the Oxford Chair of Poetry,[1] and in 1892 he was asked by a member of Gladstone's cabinet whether he would accept the laureateship if it were offered to him.[2] In both instances Morris's answer was "No".

It is evident that Morris achieved sufficient public stature to make his poetic reputation a fruitful ground for study. Only two previous attempts of any consequence have been made. Oscar Maurer, Jr., in his essay, "William Morris and the Poetry of Escape",[3] has investigated the critical reception of *Jason* and *The Earthly Paradise*; but he overstresses, I think, the critics' appreciation of escape literature, and he neglects several other important considerations; moreover, his focus is limited to only one period of Morris's life. Karl Litzenberg, in "William Morris and the Reviews: a Study in the Fame of the Poet",[4] covers more territory, but since his study is limited to sixteen pages, he necessarily leaves much to be done in the way of a detailed analysis of the critical reaction to each of Morris's poetic works.

The value of a study of Morris's poetic reputation is twofold: it can provide the groundwork for further study of Morris's poetry, and it can add to our understanding of the critical climate for poetry in the late Victorian period—an area of knowledge which has been relatively neglected, despite its importance to an understanding of both Victorian and modern critical theory.

Although Morris died in 1896, I have extended my concern with his reputation to 1900; this not only has the advantage of neatly rounding off the century, but more important, it allows us to take into account the evaluations of Morris's poetry that were called forth by his death and thus to observe any end-of-century changes in critical attitude.

This study is an expansion of a doctoral dissertation submitted to the University of Rochester, and I appreciate the constructive suggestions I received from Professors George Ford and Richard Gollin of that institution. I also wish to acknowledge my indebtedness to the College Center of the Finger Lakes for the grant-in-aid which helped to make possible the expansion and revision of this work.

In the interest of avoiding a proliferation of notes, I have usually not footnoted quotations from Victorian periodicals but have given the date of the publication in the text.

NOTES TO PREFACE

[1] J. W. Mackail, *The Life of William Morris* (London, 1899), I, 336.
[2] *Ibid.*, II, 288. See also Wilfred Scawen Blunt, *My Diaries* (New York, 1922), Part I, p. 82.
[3] Oscar Maurer, Jr., "William Morris and the Poetry of Escape", *Nineteenth-Century Studies*, ed. Herbert Davis *et al.* (Ithaca, N. Y., 1940), pp. 247-76.
[4] Karl Litzenberg, "William Morris and the Reviews: A Study in the Fame of the Poet", *RES*, XII (1936), 413-28.

CONTENTS

Preface v
1. Introductory: Truth or Beauty? 1
2. The Pre-Raphaelite Poet 17
3. The Victorian Chaucer 35
4. The Bard of the North 59
5. The Socialist Poet 81
6. The Prose Poet 103
7. Morris and the Reviewers 115
Bibliography 127
Index 133

1. INTRODUCTORY: TRUTH OR BEAUTY?

In 1834, the year William Morris was born at Walthamstow, Henry Taylor published his poetic drama, *Philip Van Artevelde*. In the famous Preface to this work, Taylor states the case for Truth as the formal end of poetry. Rejoicing that the heyday of the Romantic Movement appears to be over and that the pendulum seems to be swinging back toward "intellectual" poetry, Taylor states that he admires the imagination of the Romantics—he is speaking especially of Byron and Shelley—but finds their poetry deficient in subject-matter.

> A feeling came more easily to them than a reflection, and an image was always at hand when a thought was not forthcoming. Either they did not look upon mankind with observant eyes, or they did not feel it to be any part of their vocation to turn what they saw to account. It did not belong to poetry, in their apprehension, ... seeing all things, to infer and to instruct: on the contrary, it was to stand aloof from everything that is plain and true; to have little concern with what is rational or wise; it was to be, like music, a moving and enchanting art, acting upon the fancy, the affections, the passions, but scarcely connected with the exercise of the intellectual faculties.

This kind of poetry, lacking the control of reason, may give a brief sense of satisfaction, according to Taylor, but because it has no relevance to the reader's life, "it will not take permanent possession of the strongholds of fame"; and he advises poets to make reason the "equipoise" of imagination.[1]

The case for Beauty, against which Taylor was reacting, had been clearly stated by Arthur Henry Hallam three years earlier. In his review of Tennyson's *Poems, Chiefly Lyrical* (1830) in the *Englishman's Magazine* of August, 1831, Hallam says:

It is not true ... that the highest species of poetry is the reflective; it is a gross fallacy, that because certain opinions are acute or profound, the expression of them by the imagination must be eminently beautiful. Whenever the mind of the artist suffers itself to be occupied, during its periods of creation, by any other predominant motive than the desire of beauty, the result is false in art.[2]

But Taylor was correct in assuming that the star of didactic poetry was in the ascendant and that of a poetry of feeling and imagination, free of instructional purpose, was on the wane. Enjoying the acclaim of the public at the time, in addition to Taylor, were such poets as James Montgomery, whose voluminous productions in both verse and prose all tended to edification in the Protestant religious tradition;[3] Philip James Bailey, whose lengthy *Festus* (1839), a reworking of the Fause legend, contained "a summary of the world's combined moral and physical conditions, estimated on a theory of spiritual things", according to the author's Preface to the Fiftieth-Anniversary Edition;[4] and Martin Farquhar Tupper, who published the first installment of his platitudinous *Proverbial Philosophy* in 1838.[5] R. H. Horne's *Orion* (1843), modeled on Keats' *Hyperion*, showed a Keatsian concern for Beauty but diluted it with instructive allegory.[6]

The only important poets producing purely aesthetic poetry in the Thirties and Forties were Tennyson and Browning. Tennyson's poetic instincts were in agreement with Hallam, so that he could compose such exotic pieces as "The Sea-Fairies" (1830) and "The Lady of Shalott" (1832) and insist, in "The Poet's Mind" (1830), on the poet's right to ignore everything but his vision of beauty. But his moral sense, even in 1830, told him he ought to be concerned with human problems, as we can see from his expression, in "The Poet," of the vatic function of poetry.

This vacillation between the aesthetic and the didactic view of art appears most clearly in "The Palace of Art" (1832), in which Tennyson considers both concepts and makes a choice—or seems to. After revelling at some length in her "Godlike isolation", the Soul becomes convinced of the evil of her position and leaves the palace for a "cottage in the vale", which symbolizes social responsibility; thus, the poem can be seen as a judgment on poets who refuse to concern themselves with social questions—"an aesthetic protest against aestheticism", in the words of Henry Van Dyke.[7] But the last stanza contains

INTRODUCTORY: TRUTH OR BEAUTY? 3

a suggestion that the Soul will return to the palace, so that the tension between aestheticism and didacticism is not really resolved—as it remained imperfectly resolved for Tennyson even after he received the laureateship in 1850. The uncertainty manifested in "The Palace of Art" is, as Paull Baum says, "symptomatic of the intellectual confusion which pursued him through the rest of his life".[8] Nevertheless, by 1842, Tennyson was leaning toward the didactic view of art, probably influenced by the unenthusiastic reception of the *Poems* of 1832 (dated 1833); and the largely favorable critical response to *Poems* (1842), with its emphasis on the importance of instruction, apparently confirmed him in this view.[9]

Browning's work likewise shows a tension between aestheticism and didacticism, although Browning's didacticism was not usually so open as Tennyson's. After his first volume, the subjective *Pauline* (1833), Browning produced dramatic monologues which are presented so objectively that they seem to be sheer contemplation, such as "Porphyria's Lover" (1836) and "My Last Duchess" (1842), but he also published, at about the same time, the moralistic *Pippa Passes* (1841). This dichotomy in Browning is clearly evident in "Fra Lippo Lippi" (1855): the painter's assertion,

If you get simple beauty and naught else,
You get about the best thing God invents (217f),

sounds like an avowal of aestheticism, but it is virtually nullified by his later comment that the world

means intensely, and means good:
To find its meaning is my meat and drink (314f).

And Browning's later work usually embodies a moral view which, though not obtrusive, can be readily seen by the reader. It is significant that his great popularity began when he published *The Ring and the Book* (1868-69). D. C. Somervell states that it was probably the religious element in Browning that accounted for his large sales after this date, and he notes that a good many clergymen were addicted to quoting Browning in their sermons.[10]

The dearth of purely aesthetic poetry during the early Victorian period was a reflection of the prevalent critical attitude toward poetry. Various scholars have observed that the assumption of economic and political power by the middle class after 1830 led to the imposition of middle-class values upon the arts; and the prime value of anything in the eyes of the middle class was its possible utility. The usefulness of poetry, as Louise Rosenblatt notes in her informative study of the "Art for Art's Sake" movement, was seen to be its great power to influence conduct; therefore, good poetry should be either instructive or inspiring, or else it should provide harmless amusement.[11] Alba Warren sums up the ideal poet, according to the early Victorian view, as "the God-gifted, heaven-sent, divinely inspired seer, the interpreter of man and nature, the living breath of his time and place, and the prophet of eternal verities and of things to come".[12]

This was the dominant critical atmosphere when William Morris was born, and when he began to write his poetry; how long and to what extent this atmosphere continued dominant in Victorian criticism of poetry, I shall attempt to show in the course of my examination of Morris's poetic reputation. The reaction to Morris's work should be especially valuable in this respect, for he was part of the antithetical aesthetic movement (with a lower-case "a") which began with Rossetti, Morris, and Swinburne and continued through the focus of Pater to its culmination in the Aesthetic Movement— often called the "Decadence"—of the closing decades of the century, a movement which included figures as different from each other as Oscar Wilde, W. B. Yeats, and Arthur Symons.

The pre-eminent distinguishing feature of aestheticism was a belief in the autonomy of art—"Art for Art's Sake". It was a categorical denial of the right claimed by Victorian society to make art the handmaiden of middle-class ideals of conduct, politics, and religion. Other ideas, evolved from this basic concept, were also embraced by aesthetic writers, especially those in the final phase, whom I shall call the Aesthetes. Dorothy Richardson enumerates some of these ideas as: one, the insistence on Beauty as the sole necessary end of art; two, an emphasis on form and technique as opposed to content; three, a tendency to "aesthetic snobbery"; four, emphasis upon the "sensuous, the emotional, and the exotic elements in art with the individual reaction as a standard and as the basis of impressionistic criticism"; five, a view of life as an art in itself; and six, "the derivative attitude of moral defiance, or immorality as revolt or protest ('life for art's sake')".[13] To these, Rose Egan adds the concept that, because the artist is concerned with his intensely individual vision, he will belong to no school.[14] And quite a few critics have recognized yet another tenet, and one which carried much weight with many Aesthetes: the desire to shock the middle class (*"épater le bourgeois"*) as part of the act of moral defiance.

All of the Aesthetes subscribed to some, and usually to most of these ideas; probably none would have agreed to all, though Oscar Wilde—whom Albert J. Farmer calls "the soul of the 'decadence'"— came close.[15] Perhaps the only one of these tenets which would not apply to Wilde is the one stated by Miss Egan, for in 1882 Wilde declared that he belonged to "the pre-Raphaelite school",[16] and later he was clearly influenced by the French Symbolists; *The Picture of Dorian Gray* (1891) manifestly owes something to Huysmans' *A Rebours*, whose hero Dorian resembles.[17] In truth, this is the one tenet whose general applicability to the Aesthetes seems open to question; it probably did exist in the minds of many, for Yeats says in the *Autobiography* that the one conviction shared by the members of the Rhymers' Club was "an opposition to all ideas, all generalisations that can be explained and debated. Symons fresh from Paris would sometimes say—'We are concerned with nothing but impressions', but that itself was a generalisation and met with stony silence."[18] But earlier in the same section, which deals with the period 1887-1891, Yeats says, "I was in all things pre-Raphaelite";[19] and we may observe that they were all, as we now see them, Aesthetes, and that, in addition to Wilde, Yeats and Symons were also influenced by the French Symbolists.

Although the Aesthetic Movement attained great notoriety—a notoriety which approached infamy with the sensational trial of Wilde in 1895—by no means did the movement encompass all of the capable writers of the period. Jerome Buckley states that the "decadents" were opposed by a "vigorous 'counter-decadent' group", which included Kipling and George Wyndham among others, and which was led by W. E. Henley.[20] (Henley, curiously enough, was himself considered a "decadent" by Arthur Symons in 1893, on the basis of his impressionistic verses *In Hospital*.)[21] And Holbrook Jackson says, "Bernard Shaw and H. G. Wells, using plays and novels for criticising morality and teaching newer modes of social life; Rudyard Kipling and William Ernest Henley using verse to stimulate patriotism; Francis Adams singing revolt; Edward Carpenter, democracy; William Watson, justice ... were as characteristic of the Eighteen Nineties as the self-centred poets and critics who clustered about the *Yellow Book* and *The Savoy*."²² The older didacticism and the new aestheticism were equally part of the literary scene, however intolerable one found the other.

Thus, aestheticism had become a recognized force by the late Eighties and the Nineties; whereas earlier devotees of Beauty such as Rossetti, Morris, and Swinburne had seemed to be little side-eddies away from the main stream, the Aesthetes formed one of the main currents of creative literature, one with its own tributaries extending back into the earlier part of the century.²³

One could trace the ultimate source of English aestheticism back to Keats and his concern with Beauty as the sufficient end of art. Wilde said in 1882, "The pre-Raphaelite school to which I belong owes its origin to Keats more than to anyone else. He was the forerunner of the school.... Burne-Jones in painting, and Morris, Rossetti and Swinburne in poetry, represent the fruit of which Keats was the blossom."²⁴ But the early aesthetic impulse in literature was overborne by the didactic during the Thirties and Forties, as I indicated earlier, and it was Rossetti who returned it to the main stream. It is principally through his influence on Rossetti, then, that Keats affected the Aesthetic Movement.

As George Ford observes, an admiration of Keats was "almost a badge of membership" for the Pre-Raphaelite Brotherhood.²⁵ Holman Hunt imparted his enthusiasm for Keats to John Everett Millais, and Rossetti's admiration for Hunt's painting, *The Eve of St. Agnes*, led him to introduce himself to Hunt, a meeting which culminated in the formation of the PRB in 1848.²⁶ But, although the Pre-Raphaelites admired Keats, they did not as a general rule follow his example in creating Beauty for its own sake; even when inspired by a poem of Keats, their paintings were usually moralistic. For example, Hunt painted *The Eve of St. Agnes* to illustrate "the sacredness of honest responsible love and the weakness of proud intemperance", which he considered to be the meaning of Keats' poem.²⁷ Rossetti was also guilty of moralizing in color; his *Girlhood of the Virgin*, in which the various depicted objects stand for qualities of the Virgin, is a prime example. The Pre-Raphaelites were indeed concerned with beauty, but it was secondary—"ornamental", as William Morris said.²⁸ What was important in the practice of the PRB, from the standpoint of aestheticism, was their refusal to follow the established conventions of art and their insistence on working in their own way. This was a step in the direction of the autonomy of art.

A further step in this direction was taken in the PRB's venture into periodical literature with *The Germ*, which lived for four issues in 1850. According to the PRB journal kept by W. M. Rossetti, the Brotherhood decided against "admitting anything at all referring to politics or religion into our magazine".[29] And the Pre-Raphaelite canon of "fidelity to Nature" became fidelity to one's own artistic vision, as we see from the first four lines of W. M. Rossetti's sonnet printed on the cover of *The Germ*:

> When whoso merely hath a little thought
> Will plainly think the thought which is in him,—
> Not imaging another's bright or dim,
> Nor mingling with new words what others taught. . . .[30]

Sincerity of artistic expression was also the theme of D. G. Rossetti's prose tale, "Hand and Soul", which appeared in the first issue. The young painter, Chiaro dell' Erma, seeks and achieves fame by his painting; becoming convinced that his aim has been selfish, he resolves to produce only those works which have "for their end the presentment of some moral greatness that should influence the beholder", and he forgets "the beauty and passion of the world". But the pictures thus produced attract no attention, for they are "cold and unemphatic; bearing marked out upon them the measure of that boundary to which they were made to conform". Their ineffectuality is starkly illustrated by the bloody feud which erupts in front of Chiaro's painted allegory of Peace. The meaning of the story is made very explicit by the painter's soul in the guise of a beautiful woman who tells him that he can best serve God by painting according to his own inclination: "What He hath set in thine heart to do, that do thou; and even though thou do it without thought of Him, it shall be well done; it is this sacrifice that He asketh of thee."[31]

In keeping with the anti-moralist message of Rossetti's moralistic story, the poems which he published in *The Germ*, such as "The Blessed Damozel" and "My Sister's Sleep", were free from the moralizing tendency of his painting; and this remained true of his later poetry as well. It was because Rossetti was basically concerned with the creation of "simple beauty and naught else" (in the words of Fra Lippo Lippi) that he was, as George Ford says, the father of the

Aesthetic Movement.[32] It seems likely that Rossetti's artistic impulse always leaned toward non-didactic art, and that his didacticism in painting was caused by the influence of other Pre-Raphaelites, especially Hunt, who was his teacher for a time; "Hand and Soul" reads like a rebellion against Hunt's concept of art, and certainly against Henry Taylor's. It is significant that *The Germ* was originally Rossetti's idea, and that most of the other Pre-Raphaelites opposed it at first.[33]

The PRB did not last long, at least as a social group, for the meetings were practically discontinued by the early part of 1853.[34] When Rossetti went to Oxford in 1856, he attracted a group of followers, often called the second Pre-Raphaelite circle, the most important of whom were Morris and Burne-Jones, as well as Swinburne, who became acquainted with the group in 1857. Under the spur of Ruskin's early books on art and architecture, Burne-Jones and Morris had in 1855 decided to take up painting and architecture respectively. Rossetti confirmed Burne-Jones in his vocation and persuaded Morris to take up painting for a time.[35]

The exact extent of Rossetti's influence on Morris's poetry and poetics is difficult to establish. Some of the poems in Morris's first volume, *The Defence of Guenevere*, have a definite Rossettian flavor, but the only trait of Morris's later work which could be ascribed to the influence of the older poet is his pictorial quality; and the same quality is to be found in the work of Chaucer and Keats, both of whom Morris acknowledged as masters,[36] and in Spenser, whose *Faerie Queene* he had read in its entirety.[37] It is probable that Rossetti encouraged the younger poet in the medievalism in which Morris had been interested since boyhood, and entirely possible that his enthusiasm for Morris's poems confirmed Morris in his decision to be a poet, even though Morris had written a few poems before he knew Rossetti.[38]

Most important from the standpoint of aestheticism, however, is the probability that Rossetti's example convinced Morris that he should write poetry merely for the aesthetic pleasure it could give, and not to "set the crooked straight". Before the two men had met, Morris already showed an affinity for purely aesthetic poetry, such as Shelley's "Skylark" and the early poetry of Tennyson; but about the same time, he and his friends at Oxford got hold of a copy of *The Germ*, according to Morris's biographer, J. W. Mackail, and "from

'Hand and Soul' and 'The blessed Damozel,' which they read and re-read for ever, Rossetti rose to a first-rank place in their list of heroes." Moreover, not long afterward, the Oxford "Brotherhood", as they called themselves (perhaps after the PRB, although the Oxford group had planned a monastic brotherhood before they were fully acquainted with the work of the Pre-Raphaelites), decided to found the *Oxford and Cambridge Magazine*, which was published throughout 1856 and was undoubtedly inspired by *The Germ*.[39] It appears, then, that Rossetti's influence on Morris was strong even before they met.

At any rate, Morris adopted the view of poetry indicated in the Apology to *The Earthly Paradise*, where he renounces the intention of singing about Heaven or Hell or of trying to reform society; and it is significant that it was Morris's poetry which prompted Pater's article in the *Westminister Review* (October, 1868), the bulk of which eventually became the essay entitled "Aesthetic Poetry" in *Appreciations* (1889) and whose concluding discourse on the necessity of burning with a "hard, gemlike flame" became the famous Conclusion to *Studies in the History of the Renaissance* (1873). Morris also influenced Swinburne and Wilde, both of whom paid him the compliment of imitation in their early verse; and Yeats's admiration of Morris's work is equally well-known.

If Rossetti and Morris presented a strong argument for purely aesthetic poetry by their example, their disciple Swinburne was for a period of time the most outspoken advocate of the autonomy of art before Pater and Wilde. Louise Rosenblatt speaks of the influence on Swinburne of French writers, especially of Baudelaire, whose *Fleurs du Mal* inspired *Poems and Ballads*,[40] but the personal influence of Rossetti and Morris can hardly be over-estimated, and it certainly was sufficient to have confirmed Swinburne in his aestheticism independently of any other influence.

The war between didacticism and aestheticism came into the open when *The Spectator* of May 24, 1862, severely reprimanded Meredith for his realistic treatment of marriage and sex in *Modern Love* and for his failure to inculcate a moral. Swinburne's letter to the editor, published June 7, 1862, challenges the assumed right of the public to dictate subject-matter and demand instruction from poets:

> There are pulpits enough for all preachers in prose; the business of verse-writing is hardly to express convictions; and if some poetry, not without merit of its kind, has at times dealt in

dogmatic morality, it is all the worse and all the weaker for that. As to subject, it is too much to expect that all schools of poetry are to be for ever subordinate to the one just now so much in request with us, whose scope of sight is bounded by the nursery walls; that all Muses are to bow down before her who babbles, with lips yet warm from their pristine pap....

This denunciation of Victorian poetics, striking as it is in its typical Swinburnian rhetoric, probably did not attract a great deal of attention. But the tempest aroused by *Poems and Ballads* (1866) undoubtedly drew attention to Swinburne's next utterance of this nature. After the first critical onslaught, spearheaded by John Morley (*Saturday Review*, Aug. 4, 1866), caused J. B. Payne to cease publication of *Poems and Ballads*, Swinburne issued the defiant pamphlet entitled *Notes on Poems and Reviews* (1866), published by John Hotten (who also took over the publication of the poems).[41] In the pamphlet, Swinburne repeats his insistence that poetry should not be concerned with teaching—"There are moral milkmen enough ... crying their ware about the streets and byways"—and that its subject-matter must not be restricted by prudish standards of taste: "And if literature indeed is not to deal with the full life of man and the whole nature of things, let it be cast aside with the rods and rattles of children." Perhaps most important, Swinburne here announces the need for criticism to judge art simply as art, as "work done for the work's sake", according to the "simple laws" of the chosen art-form.[42]

Swinburne's fullest expression of his aestheticism occurs in his essay on *William Blake* (1868). Acknowledging that great works of art have been produced in which art was combined with instruction, he denies that their artistic value depends in any way upon the implied moral. "Strip the sentiments and re-clothe them in bad verse, what residue will be left of the slightest importance to art?" In a reversal of the Ruskinian doctrine that good art can only spring from a good society, Swinburne asserts:

> The contingent result of having good art about you and living in a time of noble writing or painting may no doubt be this: that the spirit and mind of men then living will receive on some points a certain exaltation and insight ... ; will become for one thing incapable of tolerating bad work, and capable therefore of

reasonably relishing the best; which of course implies and draws with it many other advantages of a sort you may call moral or spiritual.

But, Swinburne insists, not only should the artist be free to eschew any didactic purpose, but the conscious assumption of such a purpose by the artist will be fatal to art: "Art for art's sake first of all, and afterwards we may suppose all the rest shall be added to her ... but from the man who falls to artistic work with a moral purpose shall be taken away even that which he has." It will do no good to pluck out the eyes of art and set it "to grind moral corn in the Philistine mills".[43]

Swinburne was soon forced to modify his poetics to fit his new concern with politics as it was manifested in *Songs before Sunrise* (1871). In his 1872 article on *L'Année Terrible* by Hugo, Swinburne argues against interpreting "Art for Art's Sake" in a negative sense to exclude moral, political, or religious subject-matter; however, he still maintains the positive value of the theory: the work of art must stand or fall on its artistic merit alone.[44] Thus, even though Swinburne in his later work decided to leave the Palace of Art and altered his poetic theory accordingly, he remained a staunch advocate of the autonomy of art. His occasional divergence from this viewpoint, as when he condemned Zola's *L'Assommoir* for its "physical and moral abomination" (letter to *Athenaeum*, June 16, 1877), does not diminish the importance of his contribution to English aestheticism.

But the writer whom the Aesthetes considered, above all others, to be their prophet was Walter Pater, and their book of Revelation was the *Renaissance*, which Oscar Wilde called "my golden book".[45] As Yeats says, "If Rossetti was a subconscious influence, and perhaps the most powerful of all, we looked consciously to Pater for our philosophy."[46]

It was not the body of the *Renaissance* which made the greatest impact on the Aesthetes, but the Preface and the Conclusion. The Preface advances a new critical theory—the concept that, beauty being not fixed but relative, the critic judges a work of art, not by certain artistic laws of the medium, as Swinburne held, but by the impression which the work makes on the critic. Pater quotes from "The Function of Criticism", which seems to put him in agreement with Arnold, but his immediate qualification completely twists the meaning of Arnold's phrase: "'To see the object as in itself it really is,' has been justly said to be the aim of all true criticism whatever; and in aesthetic criticism the first step towards seeing one's object as it really is, is to know one's own impression as it really is, to discriminate it, to realise it distinctly." As Geoffrey Tillotson observes, in his perceptive study of *Criticism and the Nineteenth Century*, "For Arnold the object lay in the external world sharply clear for anybody who had not blinded himself with some insular or provincial zeal or other", whereas for Pater, the essence of the object was in the individual's private impression of it.[47] This being the case, the best qualified aesthetic critic will possess not a "correct abstract definition of beauty for the intellect, but a certain kind of temperament, the power of being deeply moved by the presence of beautiful objects"—like Wordsworth's poetry, as Ruth Temple notes.[48]

But for Pater the critic's function is not only to be sensitive to impressions and to analyze them, but also to discover exactly why the work of art produces such impressions:

> ... the function of the aesthetic critic is to distinguish, to analyse, and separate from its adjuncts, the virtue by which a picture, a landscape, a fair personality in life or in a book, produces this special impression of beauty or pleasure, to indicate what the source of that impression is, and under what conditions it is experienced. His end is reached when he has disengaged that virtue, and noted it, as a chemist notes some natural element, for himself and others. ...[49]

Thus, Pater's position is not really so far away from traditional aesthetic criticism as it at first appears; if the "virtue" by which art produces the impression of beauty is something concrete enough to be isolated and noted like a natural element, the critic must really be basing his judgment on things much less slippery than his private reaction. And in discovering this "virtue", the critic is very likely to take account of what Swinburne called the "simple laws" of the art-form.

The influence of the Preface to the *Renaissance* undoubtedly was largely salutary, in that it furthered the concept of the autonomy of art, but the influence of the Conclusion was largely deleterious. In this beautiful and moving version of the *carpe diem*, many Aesthetes— especially Wilde, Johnson and Dowson—found the text for "Life for

INTRODUCTORY: TRUTH OR BEAUTY?

Art's Sake", as various scholars have noted, instead of "Art for Art's Sake". Yeats wonders whether the "attitude of mind" inspired by Pater did not cause "the disaster of my friends. It taught us to walk upon a rope, tightly stretched through serene air, and we were left to keep our feet upon a swaying rope in a storm."[50]

It is true that Pater considers art as the best stimulus to a "quickened, multiplied consciousness", but he implies that virtually any kind of sensual experience can produce the same result:

> Not the fruit of experience, but experience itself, is the end. A counted number of pulses only is given to us of a variegated, dramatic life. How may we see in them all that is to be seen in them by the finest senses? How shall we pass most swiftly from point to point, and be present always at the focus where the greatest number of vital forces unite in their purest energy?
>
> To burn always with this hard, gemlike flame, to maintain this ecstasy, is success in life.[51]

Most readers would not take the common-sense attitude of John Morley toward the Conclusion. In the *Fortnightly Review* of April, 1873 Morley says:

> Of course this neither is, nor is meant to be, a complete scheme for wise living and wise dying. The Hedonist, and this is what Mr. Pater must be called by those who like to affix labels, holds just the same maxims with reference to the bulk of human conduct, the homespun substance of our days, as are held by all people in their senses. . . . He has no design of interfering with the minor or major morals of the world, but only of dealing with what we may perhaps call the accentuating portion of life.

That Morley correctly understood Pater's attitude may be assumed from Pater's expression of gratitude to Morley for "your explanation of my ethical point of view to which I fancy some readers have given a prominence I did not mean it to have".[52] Yet the Conclusion does state that to burn "always" is success, and Pater's "fancy" apparently was justified, for he felt it necessary to omit the Conclusion from the 1877 edition (though he restored it to the 1888 edition).[53]

Looking back at the development of aestheticism, we can see the source of all the main concepts of the Aesthetic Movement. From Rossetti and Morris came the concern with pure Beauty. Swinburne added his example to theirs in his earlier poetry, and his criticism distinctly furthered the idea that the experience of art should be autonomous. From this idea, several others naturally evolved—an emphasis on form, for example, at the expense of content, a fault of which Swinburne was himself guilty in much of his poetry. From Pater, besides his emphasis on Beauty, which reinforced the influence of Rossetti, Morris and Swinburne, came impressionistic criticism and finally the concept of "Life for Art's Sake".

I have given this brief survey of the development of English aestheticism not only because Morris was a part of it, but also because the critical conflict between the continuing moralistic and the developing aesthetic views of art continued throughout the period under discussion and became an important part of the background against which the critics evaluated Morris's poetry. It will be helpful to keep this in mind during the study of Morris's poetic reputation.

NOTES TO CHAPTER ONE

[1] Henry Taylor, *Works* (London, 1883), I, vii-xiv.
[2] Arthur Hallam, *Englishman's Magazine* (August, 1831), reprinted in *Victorian Poetry and Poetics*, ed. Walter Houghton and G. Robert Stange (Boston, 1968), p. 849.
[3] Hugh Walker, *Literature of the Victorian Era* (Cambridge, 1910), p. 259.
[4] *Ibid.*, p. 346.
[5] Oliver Elton, *A Survey of English Literature, 1830-1880* (London, 1920), II, 161.
[6] *Ibid.*, II, 89.
[7] Henry Van Dyke, *Studies in Tennyson* (New York, 1920), p. 25.
[8] Paull F. Baum, *Tennyson Sixty Years After* (Chapel Hill, 1948), p. 85.
[9] Edgar Shannon, Jr., *Tennyson and the Reviewers* (Cambridge, Mass., 1952), pp. 46, 95.
[10] D. C. Somervell, "The Reputation of Robert Browning", *Essays and Studies*, XV (1929), 124-29.
[11] Louise Rosenblatt, *L'Idée de l'art pour l'art dans la Littérature Anglaise pendant la période victorienne* (Paris, 1931), pp. 29-34.
[12] Alba Warren, Jr., *English Poetic Theory, 1825-65* (Princeton, 1950), p. 216.
[13] Dorothy Richardson, "Saintsbury and Art for Art's Sake in England", *PMLA*, LIX (March, 1944), 244.
[14] Rose Egan, *The Genesis of the Theory of "Art for Art's Sake" in Germany and England*, Part II, in *Smith College Studies in Modern Languages*, V (April, 1924), no. 3, p. v.

INTRODUCTORY: TRUTH OR BEAUTY?

[15] Albert J. Farmer, *Le mouvement esthétique et "décadent" en Angleterre* (Paris, 1931), p. 123.
[16] Stuart Mason, *Bibliography of Oscar Wilde* (London, 1914), p. 326.
[17] Graham Hough, *The Last Romantics* (London, 1949), p. 195.
[18] W. B. Yeats, *Autobiography* (New York, 1938), p. 145.
[19] *Ibid.*, p. 100.
[20] Jerome Hamilton Buckley, *William Ernest Henley* (Princeton, 1945), pp. vii, 152.
[21] Arthur Symons, "The Decadent Movement in Literature", *Harper's New Monthly Magazine*, LXXXVII (November, 1893), 867.
[22] Holbrook Jackson, *The Eighteen Nineties* (London, 1913), p. 34.
[23] Rosenblatt, pp. 243-44.
[24] Mason, p. 326.
[25] George Ford, *Keats and the Victorians* (New Haven, 1944), p. 107.
[26] W. Holman Hunt, *Pre-Raphaelitism and the Pre-Raphaelite Brotherhood* (New York, 1905), I, 103-5.
[27] *Ibid.*, I, 85.
[28] "The English Pre-Raphaelite School", in May Morris, *William Morris, Artist, Writer, Socialist* (Oxford, 1936), I, 302.
[29] Entry for Nov. 6, 1849, *Praeraphaelite Diaries and Letters*, ed. W. M. Rossetti (London, 1900), p. 228.
[30] Quoted by Hough, p. 54.
[31] D. G. Rossetti, *Works*, ed. W. M. Rossetti (London, 1911), pp. 549-55.
[32] Ford, p. 95.
[33] D. G. Rossetti, *Family Letters* with a *Memoir* by W. M. Rossetti (London, 1895), I, 149-50.
[34] *Praeraphaelite Diaries*, p. 308.
[35] Mackail, *The Life of William Morris*, I, 46, 106.
[36] *Ibid.*, I, 200; and *The Earthly Paradise*, Epilogue.
[37] William Morris, *Collected Works*, ed. May Morris (London, 1910-15), XXII, xxxi.
[38] Mackail, I, 51, 108.
[39] *Ibid.*, I, 67-71, 88-89.
[40] Rosenblatt, pp. 148-58.
[41] *Ibid.*, pp. 125-26.
[42] A. C. Swinburne, *Complete Works*, ed. Edmund Gosse and Thomas Wise (London, 1926), XVI, 363-73.
[43] *Ibid.*, XVI, 134-38.
[44] Swinburne, *Essays and Studies* (London, 1875), pp. 41-43.
[45] Yeats, p. 114.
[46] *Ibid.*, p. 257.
[47] Geoffrey Tillotson, *Criticism and the Nineteenth Century* (London, 1951), p. 108.
[48] Ruth Temple, "The Ivory Tower as Lighthouse", *Edwardians and Late Victorians*, ed. Richard Ellman (New York, 1960), p. 35.
[49] Walter Pater, *The Renaissance* (London, 1925), pp. viii-x.
[50] Yeats, p. 257.
[51] Pater, p. 236.
[52] Frances W. Knickerbocker, *Free Minds: John Morley and his Friends* (Cambridge, Mass., 1943), p. 194.
[53] *Victorian Poetry and Poetics*, ed. Houghton and Stange, p. 737, note 13.

2. THE PRE-RAPHAELITE POET

William Morris first discovered his great facility in verse-writing during his last year at Oxford, sometime early in 1855; he did not have to wait long to see his work in print. That fall, the Oxford "Brotherhood", which included Morris, Burne-Jones, R. W. Dixon, Cormel Price, Valentine Prinsep, and William Fulford, founded the *Oxford and Cambridge Magazine*, and the first issue appeared in January 1856. During the year of the magazine's existence (at Morris's expense), it carried three articles, eight prose tales, and five poems by Morris. The articles and tales were of little significance, and Morris abandoned prose as a vehicle for twenty years; but the publication of the poems marked the beginning of Morris's illustrious poetic career; four of them were good enough to be included in his first volume of poetry, which appeared in March 1858.[1]

Besides the poems from the magazine, *The Defence of Guenevere* contained one other poem which had appeared previously: Bell and Daldy, the publishers of *Guenevere*, had issued "Sir Galahad, a Christmas Mystery" by itself earlier in the year.[2] The poems in the volume fall loosely into two classes: the narrative and dramatic poems based on Malory's *Morte d'Arthur* or on Froissart's *Chronicles*, such as the title-poem and "The Haystack in the Floods"; and the exotic fantasies such as "The Blue Closet" and "The Tune of Seven Towers". The first group, in its crystallization of dramatic incident and revelation of character, shows the influence of Robert Browning, to whose work Rossetti had introduced Morris "after the Tennyson period";[3] and the second group, in its color-effects, its presentation of exotic situations, and its evocation of moods, shows influence by Keats and the early Tennyson, but most of all by Rossetti, to whom Morris dedicated the volume and whose paintings had inspired the two fantasy poems named above. This group represents a transitory interest with Morris, whereas the narrative and dramatic poems, which constitute the real worth of the volume and several of which rank with the best he ever wrote, reveal Morris's life-long interest in meaningful story.

The publication of *Guenevere* made a very small splash in the literary pond, nor was it much read afterward. The first edition of 500 copies was not exhausted when *The Life and Death of Jason* appeared nine years later, and after the popularity of *Jason* and *The Earthly Paradise* justified a second edition of *Guenevere* in 1875, this was apparently sufficient to satisfy the appetites of poetry-lovers until the Kelmscott Press edition of 1892.[4] Mackail's statement that the book "did not even gain the distinction of abuse: it simply went unnoticed",[5] is not quite literally true, but it accurately suggests the indifference with which it was greeted. During 1858, *Guenevere* was reviewed by only five literary journals, which devoted a total of less than eight pages to it; in June, 1860 John Skelton tried to rescue the book from obscurity, but it was not mentioned again by any of the important journals until the publication of *Jason* seven years later.

Of these six reviews, half were favorable (the *Tablet*, the *Literary Gazette*, and *Fraser's*), and half were unfavorable (the *Spectator*, the *Athenaeum*, and the *Saturday Review*). But the virulence of the latter surpassed the enthusiasm of the former. The reason appears to have been Morris's association with the Pre-Raphaelite school—instead of criticizing the book as poetry, the reviewers criticized it as the representative of a distasteful school of painters.

The PRB pictures had been well-received in 1849, but when the meaning of the insignia had been made public (through Rossetti's having confided in the sculptor Alexander Munro, who gave the information to a journalist), they were subjected to a roaring fusillade of abuse. The opening shot was fired by the *Athenaeum* (April 20, 1850) at Rossetti's *Ecce Ancilla Domini*, displayed at the National Institution, in a fierce attack that provoked Rossetti to reply in a scathing letter which the editor declined to print; but the abuse became general and increased in ferocity with the opening in May of the Royal Academy Exhibition, where Hunt's and Millais's paintings appeared.[6] The immediate hostility of the art critics was based largely on a misunderstanding of the aims of the PRB: they thought that the young painters were intent on imitating the forerunners of Raphael—and imitating not only virtues but faults—and that they refused to acknowledge the worth of any later art. It was felt that the Pre-Raphaelites were obstinately defying recognized principles of beauty and were puffed up with a conceited regard for their own ability to be arbiters of taste.[7]

In the spring of 1851, the violence of the onslaught increased until Ruskin, at the request of Coventry Patmore, came to the defence of the PRB in two letters to the *Times* and in the pamphlet, *Pre-Raphaelitism*.[8] Oswald Doughty says that Ruskin's influence decisively won the day for the PRB,[9] and W. M. Rossetti's journal entry for Jan. 23, 1853, reads: "Our position is greatly altered. We have emerged from reckless abuse to a position of general and high recognition, just so much qualified by adverse criticism as suffices to keep our once would-be annihilators in countenance."[10]

Although the battle would thus appear to have been over by 1853, it was refought, on a smaller scale, when *Guenevere* appeared five years later. Five of the six reviews referred specifically to Morris's connection with the Pre-Raphaelites, usually calling him the "poet of Pre-Raphaelitism", and all of them used some of the terms which had filled the air during the PRB controversy. Some of the most common charges against the Brotherhood had been that they imitated painters before Raphael, they were preoccupied with medieval subjects, their color was crude, and their "fidelity to nature" degenerated into caricature through extravagant attention to detail.[11] All of these charges were applied to *Guenevere* by the condemnatory reviews, and the fourth charge was at least partially acknowledged by two of the laudatory reviews.

Both the *Spectator* and the *Athenaeum* accused Morris of imitating the faults of his predecessors. The reviewer for the *Spectator* of Feb. 27, 1858, in the single paragraph which he considers sufficient to dispose of *Guenevere*, says, "Mr. Morris imitates little save faults. He combines the mawkish simplicity of the Cockney school with the prosaic baldness of the worst passages of Tennyson, and the occasional obscurity and affectation of plainness that characterize Browning and his followers." Henry Chorley, the *Athenaeum's* prolific critic of art, music and literature,[12] displays his usual conservative bias in the issue of April 3, 1858, when he centers on Tennyson's "Lady of Shalott" as the "point of departure" for all the poems in the book, thus ignoring the narrative and dramatic poems: "The 'Lady of Shalott's' loom was not a *Jaquard* machine, into which

... a few more perforated cards could be introduced, and her web, and its patterns and devices be thereby complicated." But Joseph Knight,[13] in the *Literary Gazette* of March 6, 1858, refutes the charge of imitation, although he recognizes the influence of Rossetti and Browning on a "writer of real original genius"; far from imitating Tennyson, according to Knight, Morris has not even been influenced by him:

> The difference between the two poets obviously is that Tennyson writes of mediaeval things like a modern and Mr. Morris like a contemporary. Tennyson's "Sir Galahad" is Tennyson himself in an enthusiastic and devotional mood; Mr. Morris's is the actual champion, just as he lived and moved and had his being some twelve hundred years ago.

Morris must have been gratified by this statement, for he had once told R. W. Dixon that "Tennyson's Sir Galahad is rather a mild youth".[14] The *Literary Gazette*, which had drastically declined in prestige since its heyday of the Twenties and Thirties, demonstrated in this instance that it could still display the kind of critical insight for which it had been famous earlier.[15]

On Morris's medievalism, the reviews were evenly divided: the attackers considered it an affectation and an evasion of the poet's responsibility to deal with his own times, and the defenders praised the realism with which Morris recreated the spirit of the Middle Ages. Typical of the first viewpoint is the statement of the *Saturday Review* critic—who incidentally casts doubt on either his perception or his integrity by remarking that the *terza rima* of the title-piece is "an ugly, disjointed series of *unrhymed* triplets" (italics mine). Morris's powers (he writes on Nov. 20, 1858) though considerable, have been

> altogether spoiled and wasted by his devotion to a false principle of art. False principle, we say, because a poet's work is with the living world of men. Mr. Morris never thinks of depicting man or life later than the Crusades. With him the function of art was at an end when people began, in decent life, to read and write.

These critics were apparently unheedful of, or unconvinced by, Arnold's statement five years earlier in the Preface to his *Poems* (1853). In answer to the widespread critical disapproval "of any subjects but modern ones", Arnold argues that the "eternal objects of poetry" are human actions "possessing an inherent interest in themselves"; the most interesting actions are those "which most powerfully appeal to the great primary human affections". Since these primary feelings do not change, "the modernness or antiquity of an action ... has nothing to do with its fitness for poetical representation."[16]

Morris's own justification for his medievalism appears in his 1891 lecture on "The English Pre-Raphaelite School". Noting that a common objection to the paintings of Rossetti and Burne-Jones has been their failure to portray modern life, Morris admits that this is a shortcoming.

> But is the shortcoming due to the individual artist, or is it due to the public at large? for my part I think the latter. When an artist has really a very keen sense of beauty, I venture to think that he can not literally represent an event that takes place in modern life. He must add something or another to qualify or soften the ugliness and sordidness of the surroundings of life in our generation. That is not only the case with pictures, if you please: it is the case also in literature.

Therefore, Morris concludes, we should not blame the artist who, "since his imagination must have some garb or another, naturally takes the raiment of some period in which the surroundings of life were not ugly but beautiful".[17]

Here we can see that Morris is voicing an aesthetic view of art, whereas his attackers in the three prestigious weeklies held a didactic view, as J. D. Jump observes.[18] Arnold's view, too, is ultimately moralistic, but his theory of poetry is not narrowly didactic, for he is concerned with "the one moral impression left by a great action treated as a whole".[19] He finds the satisfaction of this requirement in Greek and Shakesperian tragedy; and, although Arnold never wrote a criticism of Morris's poetry, I think it is safe to say that he would have favorably judged such a tragedy as "Sir Peter Harpdon's End" by this criterion.

In this connection, one senses that part of what troubled the critics of *Guenevere* was the fact that its subject-matter was not suitable food for "lips yet warm from their pristine pap", in Swinburne's words. The *Saturday Review* critic comments that medieval times may have been like Morris's depictions (a nice left-handed compliment!), but it is a "mercy to be rid of them," for

> there must have been a great deal of blood as well as lances and shields in those days; and though there was a great amount of kissing, both according to the chronicles and Mr. Morris, it appears that the kissers and kissed had but little respect for the marriage service.

This "respect for the marriage service" was one of the prime concerns of the Victorian middle class. At the time of *Guenevere's* birth, the first two installments of Coventry Patmore's *Angel in the House* (*The Betrothal*, 1854, and *The Espousals*, 1856) were enjoying great popularity.[20] The reason for Angel's success, as Amy Cruse puts it, was not that the public "appreciated its philosophical subtleties and its passages of pure beauty. They bought it and read it and praised it because it glorified married love and the sanctities of wedded life."[21]

Morris's medievalism did, however, find some defenders. John Skelton (*Fraser's*, June, 1860), while conceding that Morris uses perhaps too many archaisms, nevertheless praises him for his "living insight into the thought and heart" of the Middle Ages; and the *Tablet* reviewer (April 24, 1858), in a remarkably sane observation, asserts:

> Now, the poet has this right, that, in consideration of the gift of poetry which he has received, and which he spends for our benefit, we must simply accept him as he essentially is.... our objections must not go to the very root and being of his nature and inspiration, for, had such objections prevailed, we should have been without his poem.

Morris's use of strong color received the attention of three of the six reviewers. The *Saturday Review* complains that Morris has no knowledge of "gradation of tints"; but Knight praises "Golden Wings" for its likeness in "richness of colouring" to Rossetti's paintings, and Skelton says that Rossetti excels all other contemporary painters "in the oriental richness, the vivid splendour, the intense glow which he can bring out of colours", and that Morris reproduces this effect in his poems. Both views, I think, overestimate the extent to which poetry can approximate the color-effects of painting.

One of the PRB traits which had raised the most hackles among critics was the close attention to detail, and this objection had even the sanction of Ruskin; in *Pre-Raphaelitism*, he warns the Brotherhood that they sometimes distort the total design of a picture by overcarefulness.[22] It was therefore to be expected that the critics of *Guenevere* would find the same fault with the book. The most savage expression of this objection is that of the *Saturday Review* critic (evidently a late disciple of Samuel Johnson),[23] who says that, when painters try to paint every stain on every leaf on every tree,

> they not only forget what art is, but are ignorant of what artistic imitation is. This extravagance is, we think, what Mr. Morris delights in. He works in the patient spirit of the illuminators, but then he is grotesque as well as minute and patient. All his thoughts and figures are represented on a solid plane; he has no notion of distance, or aerial perspective. . . .

One might think, on reading this, that the critic was speaking of a group of paintings. To carry the analogy between poetry and painting to the length of talking about "aerial perspective", simply because false perspective was one of the faults which had been laid at the door of the PRB, is to blind oneself to the essential difference between the methods of the two arts.

Actually, there is less ground for the charge of extravagant detail in *Guenevere* than in much of Morris's later poetry, for in *Guenevere* Morris is much more concise than he will be when he takes up the writing of long narratives. Nevertheless, two of the favorable reviews also admitted this fault in *Guenevere*; but the writers felt that it was compensated for, on the whole, by the admirable "fidelity to nature" often achieved by Morris's use of detail to create "pictorial" descriptions. Even the acid *Saturday Review* commentator admits that Morris occasionally achieves an effect that is "bright, sparkling, distinct, and pictorial".

Aside from what the reviewers considered Pre-Raphaelite traits, they found two other faults in *Guenevere*: rough prosody and obscurity. Four of the six reviews briefly pointed a finger at Morris's occasional use of poor rhymes and faulty metre—though the shortcoming was amply redeemed by the overall poetic effect in the minds of Knight and the *Tablet* reviewer. A much more grievous fault, which was almost unanimously disapproved (only the *Tablet* abstaining), was what the critics considered to be wilful obscurity. This obscurity was of two kinds: the Browningesque obscurity of the narrative and dramatic poems, which Skelton explains as arising from Morris's laudable attempt to achieve realism by using the monologue form; and the obscurity of the exotic lyrics, which Knight calls "luminous indistinctness".

From this analysis of the reviews, it seems clear that a large part of the reason for *Guenevere's* blemished reputation was Morris's Pre-Raphaelite connection. As Swinburne, in his review of Jason (*Fortnightly Review*, July, 1867), puts it, *Guenevere* "seems to have been now lauded and now decried as the result and expression of a school rather than a man, of a theory or tradition rather than a poet or student. Those who so judged were blind guides of the purblind". This is not to say that the critics would otherwise not have found objections to *Guenevere*, but it is hardly possible that the objections would have been so numerous or so violent. The reviewers would probably have taken exception to Morris's rough prosody and obscurity in any case; and it is very likely that they would have disapproved of his medievalism, since it was not used as a vehicle for moralizing—as was the case with Tennyson's *Idylls*, which appeared the following year and enjoyed great popularity.[24] That the critics would have charged Morris with imitation is doubtful, and it is very improbable that they would have complained of his "crude color" or close attention to detail.

Furthermore, it is entirely within the realm of possibility that, because of *Guenevere's* Pre-Raphaelite stigma, a number of critics, like John Parker, simply ignored the book, in preference to attracting attention to it by abuse. Parker, the editor of *Fraser's*, had seen *Guenevere* in manuscript when Morris sent him the poems for possible publication, and it is evidence of the good nature which Skelton ascribes to him that Parker even printed Skelton's article, for in a letter of May 14, 1860, to Skelton, the editor says of Morris's poems, "Surely nineteen-twentieths of them are the most obscure, watery, mystical, affected stuff possible. . . . For myself I am sick of Rossetti and his whole school. I think them essentially unmanly, effeminate, mystical, affected, and obscure."[25] It should be noted that, although Rossetti's greatest notoriety did not occur until the "Fleshly School" controversy in 1871, he was already well-known as one of the PRB and considered by many as the leader of the school. It is obviously the PRB to which Parker is referring here.

Despite the slow sales and critical neglect of *Guenevere*, there is evidence that the book was read and enjoyed by a select audience, though few, in literary circles. The Oxford "Brotherhood", of course, were very enthusiastic about Morris's poems before they were published in book form. Valentine Prinsep reminisces that the early poems, which Morris would often read aloud to gatherings of friends, "were wild bits of passion such as one expects from the young, and they exactly hit off the tone of the society at Oxford. For a man not to know what was the difference between a basnet and a salade was shameful."[26] Rossetti, of course, could hardly fail to like *Guenevere*, and Swinburne, on reading Morris's poems, "would fain be worthy to sit down at his feet".[27] Ruskin, who had met Morris and was friendly with Burne-Jones, considered the poems "most noble—very, very great indeed—in their own peculiar way".[28] Another acquaintance, William Bell Scott, thought *Guenevere* the most notable first volume of any poet, giving "a poetical sense of a barbaric age strongly and sharply real".[29]

Outside of Morris's circle of friends, one of his greatest admirers, as one might expect, was Robert Browning, who described *Guenevere* in his letter of Dec. 31, 1858, to W. M. Rossetti as "the only new poems to my mind since there's no telling when".[30] Another poet, Owen Meredith (Robert, First Earl of Lytton), must have been struck with the beauty of *Guenevere*, for his letter to Browning on Oct. 4, 1862, requests "the name of the Pre-Raphaelite Poet whose Poems you showed me ('three Red Roses across the moon,' etc.)."[31]

George Saintsbury and Andrew Lang read *Guenevere* in their youth, and it may well have been a contributing influence in the development of their aestheticism. Saintsbury says that he bought the book several years after its publication and "read it straight through with an ecstasy of relish not surpassed by anything I have known of the kind".[32] And Andrew Lang notes that he knew *Guenevere* by heart at St. Andrews sometime before 1867; he and some of his classmates "found in it something which no other contemporary poet possessed in the same measure: an extraordinary power in the realm of fantasy; an unrivalled sense of what was most exquisite and rare in the life of the Middle Ages".[33]

But none of these admirers reviewed the book, although some of them referred to it in print at later times, so that whatever stimulus their publicly-expressed opinions might have provided to the early sales of *Guenevere* (an imponderable in any case) was not forthcoming.

The great popularity of *Jason* (1867) and *The Earthly Paradise* (1868-70) reawakened a certain amount of interest in their forerunner. The *Times* reviewer of *Jason* is undoubtedly correct when he says of *Guenevere* on April 11, 1868, "But many, like ourselves, only heard of that volume since *Jason* has come out." It was after the publication of *The Earthly Paradise* that *Guenevere* attracted the attention of the noted parodist C. S. Calverly, who wrote a clever parody of "Two Red Roses across the Moon", substituting for the title-refrain "Butter and eggs and a pound of cheese", and ending with the line, "And as to the meaning, it's what you please."[34]

Even so, *Guenevere* never enjoyed real fame during Morris's lifetime, either with the public or with literary critics. The writer of the *Athenaeum* review of *Jason* (June 15, 1867), in a reversal of the earlier verdict of Chorley, comments that it is a proof of the vitality of true poetry that *Guenevere*, though virtually unnoticed at first, has gradually gained "an increasing audience among men of imaginative taste", but he wistfully admits that it is "still caviar to the general public". This observation is valid for the entire period up to Morris's death, and judging from the number of published references to *Guenevere*, I would add that the book was also caviar to the general run of literary critics.

To give an indication of this, of about sixty reviews and articles concerning Morris's poetry in the period from 1867 to 1877 (the year marking the end of Morris's greatest period of poetic achievement), no more than a dozen, or about one-fifth, contain even the shortest specific reference to *Guenevere*.

However, a startling reversal of this trend began in 1896, no doubt partly because of two events that occurred in that year: the publication of Morris's *Poetical Works* in ten volumes and, later in the year, Morris's death, both of which occurrences would naturally lead critics to a reconsideration of the entire body of Morris's poetry. From 1896 to 1900, *Guenevere* enjoyed more public notice (judging by number of references) than the book had received in the entire thirty-eight years preceding, and there was only a handful of commentaries on Morris's poetry which did not include at least a passing reference to *Guenevere*. This is not to say that Morris's first volume came to be widely regarded as the poet's greatest achievement, but only that the book's existence was finally recognized by the great majority of literary critics.

One of the most interesting facts revealed by an examination of some thirty-five more-than-passing references to *Guenevere* from 1867 to 1900 is that Swinburne's wish for an impartial evaluation of the book uninfluenced by its supposed connection with a school was realized to the extent that only about one-third of the commentaries referred to Morris's Pre-Raphaelite connection. Of that third, only half considered the effect of this connection to have been deleterious; and most of these adopted a much more indulgent tone than had been the rule earlier: they spoke of Morris's "Pre-Raphaelitism" as a young man's extravagance, now happily outgrown. Fairly typical of this view is the statement of Henry G. Hewlett, who, in one of the rare literary articles of the *Contemporary Review* (December, 1874), likens the early poems of Morris to PRB paintings and repeats the conventional list of faults: crude color, antiquarianism, grotesqueness, and so on. "But a just and careful critic could not fail to discern that the singer was worthier than his song."

On the other hand were those who, like George Saintsbury in *Corrected Impressions* (1895), believed that Morris's Pre-Raphaelite sympathies led him to initiate, by the publication of *Guenevere*, a new Romantic movement in poetry which captured the true spirit of medievalism—a movement which, in Saintsbury's words, opened the way to one of the Paradises of Art, "to my taste, one delicious and refreshing to an extent not excelled by any other. To me personally, no other division of literature or of art has the qualities of a 'Vale of Rest' as mediaeval literature and mediaeval art have."[3 5]

Since the post-*Jason* commentaries which refer to *Guenevere's* Pre-Raphaelitism divide quite evenly on the worth of the book, I shall include them with the others in making a detailed analysis of the whole body of *Guenevere* criticism from 1867 to 1900. Of special interest is the fact that the early charge of imitation of other poets virtually disappeared in later criticism. Influences were discussed in more than a third of the commentaries, but they were usually viewed in the manner of Knight, as influences operating on an essentially original poet, not as objects of imitation. Not only was Morris no longer accused of imitating Tennyson, but Tennyson was hardly ever mentioned, even as an influence; when he was mentioned, it was most often for the purpose of comparing his medievalism with that of Morris, with the result that Morris usually won the decision, as he had with Knight, because the critics felt that Morris wrote about the

Middle Ages like an observer, whereas Tennyson wrote about them like a modern. As Annie MacDonell, in the *Bookman* of September, 1896, puts it, Morris is interested in his medieval materials for themselves, but other poets of the day use them as vehicles for lessons and morals and thus are really concerned with their own day rather than with the past.

Besides the Pre-Raphaelite influence, which has already been discussed, the main influences on *Guenevere*, according to the critics, were the same as those which Knight had identified: Rossetti and Browning. Rossetti's influence was sometimes considered as part of the Pre-Raphaelite influence, but at least as often, it was discussed apart from any mention of the PRB. In like manner, the faults associated by Knight with the influence of Rossetti and Browning—the occasional obscurity of the narrative and dramatic poems and the "luminous indistinctness" of the exotic lyrics—were also recognized by some of the later critics, but these comprised only about half of those who pointed out the influence.

This fact appears to be related to another striking reversal of an early trend: the widespread acceptance of the medievalism of *Guenevere*. Only about a tenth of the later criticism found fault with Morris for his use of medieval subjects, and this was by the same writers who condemned his Pre-Raphaelitism. The other critics either discussed the poems without mentioning, for either praise or blame, their medievalism, or, if they mentioned it, as forty percent of them did, it was to applaud Morris's success in recreating the atmosphere of the olden time.

The trend began, appropriately, with an article by Walter Pater; in the *Westminster Review* of October, 1868, Pater considers the chief value of *Guenevere* to be its refinement upon the profound medievalism "which re-creates the mind of the Middle Age", as in Hugo and Heine. (It is worth noting that Pater's reprint of the article twenty-one years later in *Appreciations* refers to *Guenevere* as the "first typical specimen of aesthetic poetry".)[36]

Part and parcel of the medievalism admired by Pater is what Saintsbury calls "the true Romantic vague". Morris, according to Saintsbury, is the embodiment of medieval poetry as it is found in the *Romance of the Rose* and many other places—"a noise of musical instruments accompanying an endless procession of allegorical or purely descriptive imagery"—and he compares Morris with William of

Lorris, between whom and the nineteenth-century poet the only difference, besides six centuries and a single letter in the names, is "a greater genius, the Possession of a happier instrument of language, and a larger repertory of subject and style in the later singer".[37]

Perhaps the clearest statement of the truthfulness of *Guenevere's* medievalism is that made in October, 1896 by Andrew Lang in *Longman's Magazine*, which had superseded *Fraser's* in 1882.[38] Observing, like Saintsbury, that Morris and his friends brought about a fresh dawn of romanticism, he says that Morris's first poems contain "the painful doubt, the scepticism of the Ages of Faith, the dark hours of that epoch, its fantasy, cruelty, luxury, no less than its colour and passion". The "true Romantic vague" that Saintsbury speaks of is aptly illustrated by Lang's remarks about several of the poems. He finds the "astonishing vividness of the tragedy" in "Geffray Teste Noire" like that of a vision in a magic mirror; "Shameful Death" has the same "enchanted kind of presentment". Reading them is like looking through a "magic casement" on the old waves of war. In pure fantasies such as "The Wind" and "The Blue Closet", pictures seem to arise spontaneously, "like the faces and places which are flashed on our eyes between sleeping and waking".

In view of this kind of acceptance of *Guenevere's* medievalism, it is not surprising that only a few critics still complained about the obscurity of the poems. Several other early complaints persevered to the end of the century: those against Morris's use of strong color, his sometimes rough prosody, and the occasional degeneration of his close attention to detail into grotesqueness. Of these three, strong color received the least amount of reproach. About an eighth of the later commentators would have agreed with Skelton's statement in *Fraser's* (February, 1869), in which, reversing his earlier attitude toward Rossetti's and Morris's use of color, he says that some of the early poems were as "full of colour as a paintbox" because Morris shared the Pre-Raphaelite penchant for laying on color "somewhat at random". There were at least as many others, however, who shared the opinion stated in the November, 1896, issue of *Gentleman's Magazine* (edited by Joseph Knight, the early admirer of Morris)[39] that "the colour ... in most of the poems is transcendent in beauty and glow".

The occasional rough prosody and grotesqueness which earlier critics had found in *Guenevere* continued under reproach by about a fourth of the later commentators, but most of these felt that the first was redeemed by an overall poetic spirit and the second by the frequent occurrence of vivid pictorial effects, in agreement with the early favorable reviews. The *Gentleman's Magazine* writer quoted above, for instance, judges that, although *Guenevere* is in some ways "a rather ignorant work", it nevertheless "gives Morris his highest claim to rank as a poet". And H. H. Statham, in the *Edinburgh Review* of January, 1897, speaks of both weaknesses: Morris's attention to detail is sometimes "grotesque or coarse", and there are frequent "angular and halting lines"; however, he concludes that Morris's purpose was not to write fine poetry, but to tell a story effectively, throw new light on a situation, and present a vivid picture. Above all, Statham thinks, Morris has the "Homeric gift of visualizing a scene".

Statham's statement about Morris's story-telling ability is also representative of a considerable group of later critiques which recognized, as Knight had earlier, the narrative and dramatic power of some of the poems. Because of the great variety in the volume, most of the critics did not consider Morris to have been a narrative poet until he wrote *Jason*. Amy Sharp, for example, says in *Victorian Poets* (1891) that Morris "did not begin as a narrative poet";[40] and a good many others, either by drawing attention to Morris's sudden development of narrative ability in *Jason* or by simply remaining silent on the topic, appear to have shared her view. Nevertheless, about a fourth of the later commentators called attention, like Statham, to Morris's narrative and dramatic ability. Sometimes this was done in an offhand manner, as in the statement by Harry Buxton Forman in the *London Quarterly Review* of January, 1870, that the obscurity of which Morris is sometimes guilty in poems such as "The Judgment of God" "finds its preventive in direct narration", as in "The Haystack in the Floods", which is written in "Mr. Morris's own clear, objective style". At other times, this ability was viewed as the most important quality in the book, as when Thomas Bayne, in the *St. James Magazine* of January, 1878, judges the best thing in *Guenevere* to be the "decided ease and grace of narrative power, as shown, for example, in the striking poem 'The Haystack in the Floods'".

But aside from specific references to Morris's narrative and dramatic ability, there is a good deal of implicit approval of this quality contained in the fairly widespread praise by later critics of the realistic manner in which Morris revived the spirit of medievalism, and especially in the preferences which the critics indicated for individual poems. The overwhelming favorite was "The Haystack in the Floods", which fully half of the writers selected as the best poem in the book; even Amy Sharp, who does not consider Morris to have been a narrative poet in *Guenevere,* singles out this poem as the "strongest and most characteristic" of the early poems.[41] Second-place honors were shared equally by "The Defence of Guenevere" and "Sir Peter Harpdon's End";[42] and the narrative and dramatic poems as a group enjoyed a three-to-one advantage in critical preference over the lyrical fantasies. It should be noted that this last conclusion is based on a tabulation of the number of times each poem was praised; it does not indicate a clear-cut division among the later critics in approving one group or the other. Some of them, it is true, were definite in their preference for one group over the other, but others praised poems of both groups. Nevertheless, I think the deduction is valid that the statistics indicate a tacit approval of Morris's narrative and dramatic technique.

Perhaps the most important fact shown by examination of the later *Guenevere* criticism is that more than three-fourths of the commentary freely admitted *Guenevere* into the charmed circle of true poetry, worthy of honor. About a fourth of the whole even ranked the book above all of Morris's other works—Saintsbury and Lang, for example—but more than half of the critics at least judged it to be very good poetry.

One obvious reason for this major shift in critical attitude is that with the development of the Aesthetic Movement there was a widening interest in art which attempted to create a vision of beauty unshackled by any compulsion to find a "meaning" in that vision. Related to this was the decline in the pejorative connotations of "Pre-Raphaelitism"; aside from the reverence which various Aesthetes felt for the Pre-Raphaelites, there were several reasons for this decline. For one thing, with the passage of time, many people simply forgot the PRB controversy; moreover, the chief painters associated with the school eventually attained great success. Morris's own business activity undoubtedly had some influence in this direction: over the years, Morris and Co. (which began in 1861 as Morris, Marshall, Faulkner and Co.)[43] achieved a revolution in interior decorating: this, coupled with Morris's numerous lectures on the decorative arts during the last two decades of his life, caused many people to associate "Pre-Raphaelitism" with a desire to impart beauty to the everyday surroundings of life. A good illustration of this fact is the article on Morris, Rossetti, and the Pre-Raphaelite movement in the *Edinburgh Review* of April, 1900; noting that the principles of the movement "are in a fair way to become familiar to all", the writer states that one of the main ideals of Pre-Raphaelitism is the wider application of art to the common surroundings of life and that the second circle of Pre-Raphaelites, comprised mainly of Morris and Burne-Jones, is "associated by the present generation with a fashion in decorative art of which the popularity is uncontested".

What could be more utilitarian? Thus, when the average person thought of Morris as a Pre-Raphaelite in the later part of the century, the epithet was much more likely to have favorable than unfavorable connotations. This removal of the early stigma would in itself be sufficient to cause those who read *Guenevere* to do so with an unprejudiced eye.

Even so, Morris's first volume of poetry never quite achieved the stature of some of his later work in the minds of a majority of critics writing from 1858 to 1900. The disrepute into which the book had fallen in its infancy, however, was replaced by sincere veneration in its later years. *Guenevere* had finally won her case.

NOTES TO CHAPTER TWO

[1] Mackail, *Life of William Morris*, I, 51, 87-93, 135.
[2] C. E. Vaughan, *Bibliographies of Swinburne, Morris and Rossetti*, English Association Pamphlet No. 29 (December, 1914), p. 7.
[3] Morris, *Collected Works*, XXII, xxxii.
[4] Harry Buxton Forman, *The Books of William Morris Described* (London, 1897), pp. 37-41; also Vaughan, p. 7.
[5] Mackail, I, 130.
[6] W. M. Rossetti, *Memoir*, I, 161-62.
[7] Oswald Doughty, *A Victorian Romantic* (London, 1949), p. 99.
[8] *Ibid.*, pp. 109-10.
[9] *Ibid.*, p. 112.
[10] *Praeraphaelite Diaries and Letters*, ed. W. M. Rossetti, p. 306.
[11] Doughty, pp. 99, 109.
[12] Leslie Marchand, in *The Athenaeum* (Chapel Hill, 1941), p. 192, identifies Chorley as the writer of this article.

[13] May Morris identifies Knight as the author of this article, in *Collected Works*, VI, x.
[14] Mackail, I, 45.
[15] Merle Mowbray Bevington, *The Saturday Review, 1855-1868* (New York, 1941), p. 5.
[16] *Poetical Works of Matthew Arnold*, ed. C. B. Tinker and H. F. Lowry (London, 1950), pp. xix-xx.
[17] May Morris, *William Morris, Artist, Writer, Socialist*, I, 304-5.
[18] J. D. Jump, "Weekly Reviewing in the Eighteen-Sixties", *RES*, XXIV (January, 1948), 56.
[19] Arnold, *Poetical Works*, p. xxviii. Even in later years, though Arnold was against pure aestheticism, he did not avow a narrow didacticism. In his essay on "Wordsworth" (1879), he says that "the greatness of a poet lies in his powerful and beautiful application of ideas to life, to the question: How to live"—in other words, the treatment of "moral ideas"; and "a poetry of indifference towards moral ideas is a poetry of indifference towards *life*." But Arnold interprets "moral" in a larger sense than is customary; it applies, in his view, not only to Milton's "Live well; how long or short, permit to heaven" (*Paradise Lost*, XI, 554), but equally to Keats' "Forever wilt thou love, and she be fair" ("Ode on a Grecian Urn", line 20). He places Wordsworth above poets such as Burns, Keats, and Heine, not because his poetry is uniformly greater than theirs, or because it is more didactic—in fact, he calls the purely didactic poem "a lower kind" of poetry—but because Wordsworth "deals with more of *life* than they do; he deals with *life*, as a whole, more powerfully".—*Essays in Criticism*, First and Second Series (New York, A. L. Burt and Co., n.d.), pp. 353-56. It probably should be added however, that what Arnold means here by "life" is open to debate.
[20] Oliver Elton, *A Survey of English Literature, 1830-1880*, II, 99-101.
[21] Amy Cruse, *The Victorians and their Reading* (New York, 1935), p. 226.
[22] John Ruskin, *Pre-Raphaelitism* (1851), p. 51.
[23] In Johnson's *Rasselas*, Imlac asserts that the business of the poet is "to examine, not the individual, but the species; to remark general properties and large appearances; he does not number the streaks of the tulip, or describe the different shades in the verdure of the forest" (*Works*, London, 1806, VII, 332).
[24] Paull F. Baum, *Tennyson Sixty Years After*, p. 176.
[25] Skelton, *The Table-Talk of Shirley* (Edinburgh, 1896), pp. 78-79.
[26] Val C. Prinsep, "A Chapter from a Painter's Reminiscence...", *Magazine of Art*, XXVIII (February, 1904), 169.
[27] Letter to Edwin Hatch, Feb. 17, 1858, in *Swinburne Letters*, I, 15.
[28] Letter to Brownings, March 29, 1858, in *Works of John Ruskin*, ed. E. T. Cook and Alexander Wedderburn (London, 1909), XXXVI, 280.
[29] William Bell Scott, *Autobiographical Notes*, ed. W. Minto (New York, 1892), II, 42.
[30] W. M. Rossetti, *Ruskin, Rossetti, Praeraphaelitism* (London, 1899), p. 219.
[31] *Letters from Owen Meredith to Robert and Elizabeth Barrett Browning*, ed. Aurelia and J. Lee Harlan, Jr. (New York, 1936), pp. 209-10.
[32] George Saintsbury, *Corrected Impressions* (New York, 1895), p. 180.
[33] Andrew Lang, *Contemporary Review*, XLII (August, 1882), 202.
[34] C. S. Calverly, *Fly Leaves* (New York, 1872), p. 50.
[35] Saintsbury, p. 185.
[36] *Victorian Poetry and Poetics*, ed. Houghton and Stange, p. 747.

[37] Saintsbury, pp. 186-87.
[38] Walter Graham, *English Literary Periodicals* (New York, 1930), p. 291.
[39] Graham, p. 159.
[40] Amy Sharp, *Victorian Poets* (London, 1891), p. 173.
[41] *Ibid.*
[42] This evaluation has persisted, it seems. In seven or eight anthologies of recent years, these are the three poems usually printed.
[43] Mackail, I, 148.

3. THE VICTORIAN CHAUCER

After the debacle of *Guenevere*, Morris was in no hurry to publish again. He had plenty to occupy his attention: his marriage to Jane Burden in 1859, the building of Red House, the birth of his daughters—Jenny in 1861 and May in 1862—and his activity for Morris, Marshall, Faulkner and Co. from 1861 on.[1] Nevertheless, Morris found time to write a large amount of poetry during the nine years between the publication of *Guenevere* and that of *Jason*.

According to May Morris, the poet had apparently planned a complete Arthurian cycle, for he left fragments of poems on Iseult of Brittany,"The Maying of Queen Guenevere", and "Sir Palomydes' Quest";[2] this plan Morris abandoned, perhaps in part because of the poor reception of his first book, but the main reason was probably the publication of Tennyson's *Idylls* in 1859. About this same time, Morris projected a dramatic poem on the fall of Troy; of the intended twelve scenes, he completed six and left fragments of two more, comprising more than 1200 lines in all.[3] He continued to work on this project until 1862, when he apparently discarded the idea; and although Mackail says that Morris did not begin composing *The Earthly Paradise* until late in 1865, when he moved to London,[4] May Morris draws attention to a notebook dated 1861 which contains the first drafts of "The Watching of the Falcon", "The Proud King", and some verses for June and July.[5] Altogether, then, *The Earthly Paradise* was in production for nearly a decade—though there probably was a gap of several years during which Morris set poetry aside, as Mackail maintains.

Morris took the idea for the structure of *The Earthly Paradise* from Chaucer's *Canterbury Tales*, in which a group of pilgrims take turns recounting stories from various sources. In Morris's work, "certain gentlemen and mariners of Norway" flee from the plague and sail in search of the Earthly Paradise; old and disillusioned after many disappointments, they reach a western island inhabited by descendants of the ancient Greeks. Here they stay, and it is decided that twice each month the Wanderers and their hosts will attend a feast and alternate in telling stories from their respective repositories of legends. This ritual provides the backdrop against which Morris presents twenty-four tales based on classical and medieval sources.

Morris's narrative frame, except for the lengthy Prologue, receives much less attention than that of Chaucer, and Morris does not develop the characters of individual pilgrims as Chaucer does. Even in the Prologue, which is a beautiful poem in itself, there is little development of character, because, contrary to his predilection for character-revelation in some of the *Guenevere* poems, Morris is now more interested in the story than in the plumbing of character. This also holds true for most of the tales in *The Earthly Paradise*: with the notable exceptions of Medea in *Jason*, Paris and Oenone in "The Death of Paris", the title-character in "The Story of Rhodope", and Kiartan, Bodli, and Gudrun in "The Lovers of Gudrun", it can be said with a fair degree of certainty that the personages of *The Earthly Paradise* are not round, but flat—as indeed are the characters in Chaucer's individual tales, and as personages in romance have almost always been.

Another distinction between Chaucer and Morris is that their aims, though similar in the respect that both want an excuse for telling stories, are essentially different. Chaucer is basically concerned with the pilgrimage, a search for an unearthly paradise which can actually be attained; some of his tales are told simply for the entertainment of his readers, but some of them point morals which should help one toward the attainment of paradise, and some illustrate existing evils which hinder man's spiritual progress. Chaucer's assertion in taking leave of the *Canterbury Tales*, "For oure book seith, 'Al that is writen is writen for oure doctrine,' and that is myn entente",[6] may be overstated but expresses the core of the matter.

On the other hand, Morris is concerned with a search for an earthly paradise which is impossible of attainment except in the realm of art. This is what the Wanderers discover after their fruitless search; they achieve a state, not of perfect, but of near-content in listening to old stories. As Graham Hough observes, the story-telling in *The Earthly Paradise* performs the same symbolic function as Keats' Grecian urn:

it "represents art in general, the only deathless land there is"—although Hough's deduction that Morris's aesthetic would exclude tragedy does not follow.[7] Thus, Chaucer and Morris, broadly speaking, write from the moralistic and aesthetic views of art respectively. Outside of the structural similarity and the superficial likeness of Morris's using the three Chaucerian metres—heroic couplet, octosyllabic couplet, and rhyme royal—the real similarity between the two poets is simply their fondness for straightforward, unhurried narration and detailed description.[8]

The relative obscurity of Morris's poetic status ended with the publication of *Jason* (1867), which, when it grew too large for inclusion in *The Earthly Paradise*, Morris decided to issue separately;[9] and with the appearance of the latter work in four parts (1868-70), his fame was firmly established. If not quite filling the bill as bread for the masses, these poems were much more widely appreciated than caviar. For poetry, both works sold extremely well throughout Morris's lifetime. The first edition of *Jason* was sold out before the end of the year, necessitating a second edition in December; in all, the book went through nine editions (including the Kelmscott Press large quarto of 1895) before its inclusion in the *Poetical Works* (1896). *The Earthly Paradise* was even more popular: the first volume, including Parts I and II, went through four editions before the issuance of Part III in November, 1869, and a fifth edition in two volumes in 1870; Part III went through three separate editions in 1869 and 1870, and Part IV was likewise issued separately three times in 1870 and 1871; Parts I-IV were issued together six times before their inclusion in the *Poetical Works*.[10] Moreover, it is significant of the great popularity of Morris's largest poetic production that virtually every book he published thereafter carries on the title-page the notation that it was written by the author of *The Earthly Paradise*.

In addition to this manifest acceptance by the public, *Jason* and *The Earthly Paradise* also enjoyed widespread critical popularity throughout the author's lifetime. After the appearance of the first volume of the latter work, most reviewers discussed the two works together, partly because of the stylistic similarity and partly because some of the critics correctly assumed that *Jason* was first meant to be included in *The Earthly Paradise*. From 1867 to 1872, more than forty articles in literary journals contained detailed reviews of one or both books, and an overwhelming majority of them (about ninety-five percent) were predominantly favorable. Of some forty commentaries from 1873 to 1900, four-fifths were favorable, so that the two works began at the top level in the estimation of critics and ended the century at a level slightly lower but still very high.

Fully half of the articles from 1867 to 1900 compared Morris to Chaucer as a narrative poet, most of them adjudging him either a "modern Chaucer" or else the best narrative poet since Chaucer. An even larger percentage of the reviews praised Morris's story-telling ability whether or not they mentioned Chaucer; and herein, I think, lies one main reason for the great popularity of *Jason* and *The Earthly Paradise*: their narrative quality.

Beginning with the first review of *Jason* and continuing at intervals till the end of the century, reviewers applauded Morris as a narrative poet for various reasons, one of the foremost of which was the clarity of his narration. The *Athenaeum* of June 15, 1867, praises Morris as a "chronicler who has a tale to tell, the interest of which is in the events", not in the chance provided for a display of imagination. The warm welcome accorded to *Jason* by this important critical review irritated Edward Fitzgerald, who exclaimed bitingly about the *Athenaeum's* treating Morris, Rossetti, and Browning as poets scarcely inferior to Dante and Shakespeare.[11] But the *Athenaeum* was by no means alone in its approval of Morris's poetry.

The *Times* of April 11, 1868, lauds *Jason* because its figures are "vividly dramatic, with no self-explanation, no self-consciousness", and the *Spectator* of March, 1870, in an article which expiates the journal's earlier sin against *Guenevere*, says, "It has become a new thing that beauty should be offered without mystery and apprehended without effort." Later in the period, Annie MacDonell, in the *Bookman* of September, 1896, considers the crowning quality of Morris's work to be its lucidity, that which, "for a narrator there is no better". And a *Spectator* critique of the same month (Sept. 12, 1896) is just as clear in praising what Morris does *not* do: "hide a lack of thought under enigmatical language". In short, the tone of about twenty commentaries, of which these five seem fairly typical, is that Morris's clear narrative style was a relief from the obscurity of much contemporary poetry, the same kind of obscurity which had been reproved in *Guenevere*.

Closely allied to the quality of clarity is the "unconsciousness" or objectivity of Morris's narrative style. The *Spectator* of June 20,

1868, rejoices, "There is nothing more delightful than to escape from the problem-haunted poetry of the day into the rippling narrative of Mr. Morris's fresh and vivid fancy." Poetry-lovers are "over-wearied with an excess of subjective verse", complains the *Fortnightly Review* of June, 1868, and the writer welcomes Morris as a poet whose "central quality is a vigorous and healthy objectivity". (The approval of the liberal *Fortnightly* is not surprising, in view of the fact that its editor, John Morley, knew Swinburne at Oxford and may have met Morris and Rossetti when they were painting the Oxford Union hall.)[12] Similarly, *Blackwood's* (July, 1869) expresses special admiration for "Mr. Morris's boldness" in refusing to conceal "his love for the objective, in deference to a presumed love for the subjective on the part of his audience"; to Morris, says the writer, "a story of the olden time is dear for its own sake", not as a "vehicle for subtle analysis of motive, or as an introduction to philosophical reflections".

Equally telling evidence of the desire for objectivity on the part of critics is the fact that in several instances the same writers who praised Morris's unconsciousness in *Jason* and the first volume of *The Earthly Paradise* lamented what they considered his subjectivity or self-consciousness in some of the poems in Parts III and IV. For example, the *Blackwood's* review of Part III (May, 1870), probably written by the author of the article just quoted, criticizes "The Story of Rhodope" because Rhodope is not a classical maiden, "but a much-musing modern one, thinking upon her thought, and considering her fate almost as much as if she had been the heroine of a new novel." This, the reviewer thinks, is much less desirable than the "unquestioning directness and simplicity" with which Morris presented the heroines of his earlier tales, such as Atalanta. And Sidney Colvin, in the new-founded (1869) but already respected *Academy*[13] (Dec. 15, 1870), notes that, whereas in the beginning it seemed that Morris was content with the simplest elements of story-telling—"a new thing in modern literature"—other elements have crept into Parts III and IV: "deeper poetical motive, greater complexity of incident, greater force and subtlety of emotion, more of the conscious and sensitive modern self mingling with the ancient direct nature and all-adorning fancy. And with these has come the loss of something of the old melodious equality, and gentle maintenance of delightfulness."

An especially welcome aspect of Morris's direct, objective manner of story-telling, in the opinions of some reviewers, was its freedom from moralizing. Thus, the *Saturday Review* of May 30, 1868, in a reversal of its prudish attitude toward *Guenevere*, views *The Earthly Paradise* as a relief, not only from subjective verse, but from the mass of "moralistic" and "disquisitional" poetry of the day. And the *Spectator* review of Volume I (June 20, 1868) voices satisfaction that Morris avoids preaching even indirectly, shunning "the covert satire of the modern style". Or, as Andrew Lang puts it, in the *Contemporary Review* of August, 1882, "In modern poetry ... the temptation to 'find a moral everywhere,' as the Duchess does in *Alice in Wonderland*, is certainly great", but Morris never points a moral, "though everyone who chooses may deduce, from tales like *Bellerophon* and *The Man Born to be King*, the value of courage, probity, and good humour."

There were other reviewers, however, who were not so happy with Morris's abstinence from moralizing and who would, in fact, have preferred to see the poet assume the role of teacher. For example, Henry Alford, in the *Contemporary Review* of August, 1868, hopes that the next volume of *The Earthly Paradise* will be "as delightful as this one" but suggests that, after this work is finished, the author would be well-advised to adopt a loftier aim: "Out of the Christian treasures of the Middle Ages, why not select some theme which shall go to the heart, as well as enchant the ear? Might not the 'Earthly Paradise' lead on to a greater work with a more glorious epithet still?" The *Christian Observer* of March, 1870, as might be expected from its title, is less complimentary and more insistent that the poet should don the robes of the teacher: speaking of the poems in *The Earthly Paradise*, the writer complains that, in answer to those "who ask *Cui bono?* we fear our verdict must be an unfavourable one. We seek in vain through them for any high or holy lesson taught, anything which can, in any shape or way, lift the soul from earth to heaven."

Morris did not lack defenders, however; aside from those reviewers who found Morris's poetry a relief from the prevalent moralizing tendency, there were a few who ventured to state explicitly that Beauty, without Truth, was sufficient to confer nobility on a poem which possessed it. Arthur Quiller-Couch says in the *Speaker* of Oct. 10, 1896, that those who consider Morris's poetry empty because it does not instruct are wrong, for it is "full of beauty, beauty beloved for its own sake, and therefore a hundred times more instructive to the prepared understanding than the squalid novels" in which these critics find reading to their mind. Poetry, he asserts, "is sufficiently justified if it please ... by any genuine beauty". Oscar Wilde, in *The English Renaissance of Art* (1882), goes even further: not only is beauty a sufficient justification for poetry, he says, but it is the *only* justification. The true poet will allow nothing debatable to enter the "sacred house of Beauty"; if he wants to write about the problems of the day, "it will be, as Milton nobly expressed it, with his left hand, in prose and not in verse"; and Wilde extols *The Earthly Paradise* as a poem in which the spirit of beauty is "the one dominant note".[14]

The other common defence which was offered by Morris's admirers on this score was a tacit assent to the critical dictum that great poetry should be instructive; that is, they pointed out that Morris's poems were, after all, instructive, albeit not obtrusively so. Thus, the *Athenaeum* review of Part III (Dec. 25, 1869) notes with satisfaction that the moral of "The Man Who Never Laughed Again" is "finely worked out". Likewise, the *Saturday Review* of May 30, 1868, points out that Morris has developed "beautifully and tellingly that strange foreshadowing of redemption and a Redeemer which is partially vouchsafed in the legend of Alcestis"; and in the issue of Dec. 11, 1869, the same journal protests against those who say that *The Earthly Paradise* is entirely "of the earth earthy", because it "will to rightly-strung hearts suggest the lesson of not resting in things sublunary" and thus indirectly "subserves a higher and loftier purpose".

On the related question of delicacy or indelicacy in the treatment of sex, about an eighth of all the reviews commented, and they were evenly divided. A few writers associated Morris with "Swinburnianism" (e.g. *Saturday Review* of Dec. 24, 1870) and, after Buchanan's notorious attack in the *Contemporary Review* of October, 1871, with the "fleshly school of poetry". But defenders quickly arose and pointed out the tact with which Morris treated sex, even when dealing with the amours of the gods, which the ancient Greeks had treated with what moderns would consider brutal frankness.

In this connection, it may be worth digressing to note that Morris's treatment of love is sensual and sometimes very suggestive but not usually as thorough-going in its fleshliness as that of Rossetti and Swinburne. Take, for example, "Troy Town" from Rossetti's *Poems* (1870), in which Helen compares her breasts to apples,

> "Grown to taste in the days of drouth,
> Taste and waste to the heart's desire:
> Mine are apples meet for his mouth!" (59ff)

And "Laus Veneris", in Swinburne's *Poems and Ballads* (1866), contains quite a number of very concrete details such as

> Below her bosom, where a crushed grape stains
> The white and blue, there my lips caught and clove ... (166f)

Morris does not shy at connecting lips with bosoms, but he will simply say it happened, without going into detailed food imagery—as in "The Doom of Acrisius", where he says Danaë trembled

> To Feel the loving hands of mighty Jove
> Draw down her hands, and kisses on the head
> And tender bosom....[15]

A final reason for the general approval of Morris's use of the narrative form was its value as wholesome entertainment; it provided a refreshing escape from the worldly cares of the day. A goodly number of critics took Morris at his word that he was an "idle singer of an empty day", striving to "build a shadowy isle of bliss / Midmost the beating of the steely sea". For instance, G. H. Lewes, who used to read *The Earthly Paradise* with George Eliot during their morning stroll, advised John Blackwood, "*If ever* you have an idle afternoon bestow it on the 'Earthly Paradise'".[16] The public expression of this viewpoint is fairly represented by the following two citations. The *Spectator* of March 12, 1870, states that, although the noblest poetry is that which strengthens us "to look at doubt and danger with steadfast eyes" and arms us "with exalted hope and renewed faith in good", there comes a time when we would rather forget our cares than learn how to face them, and the poet "who can teach us the right and innocent forgetfulness has surely attained high praise". And Thomas Bayne, in the *St. James Magazine* of January, 1878, puts it as Morris himself might have done: "Is it not the case that the world—all that roar of machinery and that bustle about wealth—is too much with us?" There is a crying need for "cultured repose", Bayne asserts, and Morris is performing "a distinct and notable service when he provides one possible means of escape".

From the foregoing examination, it seems clear that the principal reasons for the critical welcome extended to Morris as a reviver of the art of the gestour were the reaction against obscurity, self-consciousness and didacticism in the verse of the day on the one hand, and the desire for escape or "cultured repose" on the other. This is not to suggest that these were the only reasons for the popularity of *Jason* and *The Earthly Paradise* or even that reviewers who praised the two books for these reasons found no fault with them on other scores. However, since half of all the detailed commentary from 1867 to 1900 connected the names of Morris and Chaucer, it would perhaps be best at this time to analyze in detail the comparisons of the two poets; in the course of this analysis, some of the other points of praise and blame will fall into place, and the rest may be deferred until later.

An obvious point of similarity between Morris and Chaucer was the modern poet's use of Chaucerian metres, but only about a tenth of the reviewers drew attention to it—perhaps thinking it too obvious to mention—and three-fourths of these spoke favorably of it. W. J. Courthope, in the *Nineteenth Century* of February, 1897, reproves Morris for using Chaucer's verse-forms because they do not spring "naturally out of the idiom of his time"—as if Chaucer's contemporaries spoke in rhyme royal or couplets! And the *Quarterly Review* (not to be confused with the *London Quarterly Review*) of January, 1872 disapproves of Morris's having set aside the heroic couplet (the closed couplet of Dryden) in favor of Chaucer's more "elementary style" and observes that Morris shows even less respect for the couplet than Chaucer, who at least did not break it in the middle of the line. But this was the very reason for praise among the rest of the critics who mentioned this feature. Typical is George Saintsbury's admiring statement in *Corrected Impressions* (1895) that Morris did to the heroic couplet what Milton and Wordsworth did to blank verse: "He broke it up, changed its centres of gravity, subjected it to endless varieties of *enjambement*."[17]

Morris's least superficial Chaucerian trait, and one which was acknowledged by virtually all who made the comparison, was his leisurely, straightforward method of narration—a quality which, as I have indicated, met with widespread appreciation. An essential element in this revival of the gestour's art is an unquestioning acceptance of the "givens" of the story being told; this acceptance, variously identified by the critics as "the spirit of wonder", "naiveté", or "childlike implicitness of belief", was plentifully recognized as a vital part of Morris's method. For example, the *Spectator* review of *Jason* (June 15, 1867) says:

> It is no small thing for a poet of our own day to make such a subject as this live again with real vividness before the eyes, to write of the recovery of a golden fleece, and the yoking of brazen bulls which spurted fire from their throats, with the old ardour of belief, and never raise a smile even at the childishness of the old story.

And Harry Buxton Forman, in the *London Quarterly Review* of January, 1870, states that Morris and Chaucer stand apart from all other English poets in showing complete sympathy with the stage of human development concurrent with the supposed time of the story—a statement which I think applies more to Morris than to Chaucer (The "Knight's Tale", for instance, supposedly takes place in ancient Greece, but sounds more like a story of medieval chivalry).

This "most indispensable quality in simple tale-telling", according to Forman, is accomplished partly by a plain statement of the supposed events and partly by "ingenuous minuteness of circumstantial details". Forman points especially to the objective method by which Morris introduces gods, giving physical symptoms of their approach and departure. One of Forman's examples is the incident in "Atalanta's Race", after Milanion's vigil in the Temple of Venus, when the mysterious approach of the goddess is indicated by the lover's physical sensations: he sees a bright cloud enter the temple and smells "delicious unnamed odours" as the cloud surrounds him and makes him faint;

> At last his eyes were cleared, and he could see
> Through happy tears the goddess face to face
> With that faint image of Divinity....

And when she vanishes, the three golden apples remain in witness of her visit.

John Skelton, one of the few early defenders of *Guenevere*, also speaks admiringly of Morris's realistic treatment of the antique supernatural. Writing in *Fraser's* (February, 1869), Skelton singles out Jove's visit to Danaë in "The Doom of King Acrisius" as an effective combination of concrete detail and suggestion of godhood. As Danaë stands at the window watching the dawn, the sunbeams grow more yellow, "not whiter as their wont is", and she hears a tinkling sound while being showered with liquid gold which trickles down her body—strangely, Skelton seems not to notice the erotic suggestiveness of this imagery; at the god's departure, his divinity is underscored by a natural phenomenon: "And loud it thundered from a cloudless sky." Quite a few other reviewers also commended Morris's objective method of dealing with the supernatural, and they frequently used the same examples as Forman and Skelton.

But Morris did not restrict the use of concrete detail to making the supernatural believable, as the critics recognized. He used it throughout the poems with the effect of rendering all the events in the stories vivid and credible, and a number of critics viewed this faculty as an especially felicitous result of the Chaucerian influence. Typical is the approving comment of the *Saturday Review* (May 30, 1868) that both the classical and the medieval tales in *The Earthly Paradise* have "that portrayal of life in detail" which was an express feature of the gestour's art "and which Chaucer imaged so truly".

Much of the detail in *Jason* and *The Earthly Paradise* is concerned with natural description, and the reviewers were lyrical in their praise of this aspect of Morris's art, with scarcely a dissenting voice. Even those who found little else of value in the two books commended the descriptions of nature. For instance, an article in *Blackwood's* (July, 1899) finds fault with everything that Morris produced, either in literature or in art, but admits that *The Earthly Paradise* has one shining quality: "it is dimly pictorial; its landscapes are seen"—though even here, the writer dilutes the effect of his praise by the quibbling adverb "dimly".

Other critics were much more enthusiastic. "In his passion for Nature, Mr. Morris is a painter", says the *Athenaeum* review of *Jason* (June 15, 1867), and this was the tenor of commentaries on both books throughout the period under discussion. Although most critics looked on *Jason* as a new departure which signified Morris's escape from Pre-Raphaelite influence, some of them used the Pre-Raphaelite motto, "fidelity to Nature", to describe the felicity of Morris's natural descriptions, and almost all of them referred to such passages as pictorial. Swinburne, in his review of *Jason* (*Fortnightly Review*, July, 1867), warmly commends the "faithful touches" in which "no flower of the landscape is slurred, but no flower is obtrusive; the painting is broad and minute at once, large and sure by dint of accuracy". Pater, in the *Westminster Review* (October, 1868), suggests that Morris went directly to nature for some of his descriptions (a regular practice among Pre-Raphaelite painters), for he considers one of Morris's "charming anachronisms", by which he vitalizes an ancient subject and keeps from being merely antiquarian, to be the "sense of English scenery" which Morris imparts to his poetry. Other writers were more specific: the *Fortnightly Review* (June, 1868) asserts that no other modern English poet "has so possessed this excellent gift of looking freshly and simply on external nature in all her many colours, and of reproducing what he sees with such effective precision and truthfulness". And Harry Buxton Forman, in his *London Quarterly Review* article (January, 1870), says Morris's landscapes are "far too fresh . . . to be conceivably the result of a second-hand study".

But there were other critics who, granting that Morris probably drew some of his scenes from nature, judged that he also drew some from imagination (as he drew details of action and costume) and that he achieved "fidelity to nature" in these as well. Thus, the *Athenaeum* of Dec. 25, 1869, says of "The Man Who Never Laughed Again" that "the descriptions possess that striking verisimilitude which gives Mr. Morris a special position amongst poetic narrators", and the writer adds, "The fidelity of Mr. Morris to outward life and nature becomes all the more vivid by the co-operation of his fancy."

The pictorial quality of Morris's poetry was not restricted, however, to landscape painting. Probably few critics were aware of Morris's own remark that his poems, like Rossetti's, were "of the nature of a series of pictures",[18] but most of them would have assented to the justice of the comment. As we have seen, although the Pre-Raphaelite stigma prevented *Guenevere* from receiving a fair trial, its pictorial quality was admired by several of the early critics and about a fourth of the later commentators. But the stigma was not attached to the later works, and they contained more pictures, not only because they were longer, but also because they were straight narrative, instead of a mixture of narrative, dramatic, and lyrical poetry as *Guenevere* had been. It is not surprising, then, that the pictorial effects in *Jason* and *The Earthly Paradise* were appreciated by a large majority of critics.

Andrew Lang and a couple of other aesthetic critics felt that Morris's picture-making faculty had slipped a little after his first book—no doubt because the later works lacked the "true Romantic vague". In *Longman's Magazine* (October, 1896), Lang says of Morris, "His art was always pictorial, but, in *Jason* and later, he described more, and was less apt, as it were, to flash a picture on the reader, in some incommunicable way." This viewpoint, however, was overwhelmingly negated by the other critics, most of whom considered Morris's descriptive art as fine as ever, and some of whom—the critics of Morris's earlier "Pre-Raphaelitism"—thought it was better than before, because now it was purified of its earlier tendency to grotesqueness. As an example of the latter turn of mind, John Skelton, in *Fraser's* (February, 1869), says that, since Morris has been cured of his "improper love for paint", his descriptive passages are "full of light and air, due, first to the fact that he *sees* with eminent distinctness; and secondly, to the fact that the ... dominant impression is firmly and rapidly seized". From the passage in "The Man Born to be King" when Michael is riding uphill, Skelton quotes the lines,

> He saw before him, like a wall,
> Uncounted tree trunks dim and tall.

Instead of painting individual trees, Skelton says, Morris here skilfully conveys the desired impression of the woods as dark and wall-like. The example is well-chosen, and there are undoubtedly quite a few instances to which Skelton's observation applies, but there are also a great number of passages in which Morris describes "individual trees" with fully as much attention to detail as he did in *Guenevere*, and usually more. This is literally the case in "The Story of Cupid and Psyche", when Psyche awakes after having been transported by the wind to Cupid's valley:

> And all about were dotted leafy trees,
> The elm for shade, the linden for the bees,
> The noble oak, long ready for the steel
> Which in that place it had no fear to feel;
> The pomegranate, the apple, and the pear
> That fruit and flowers at once made shift to bear,
> Nor yet decayed therfor; and in them hung
> Bright birds that elsewhere sing not, but here sung
> As sweetly as the small brown nightingales
> Within the wooded, deep Laconian vales.[19]

Although Morris's use of circumstantial detail was much admired, it still attracted some brickbats. Many critics might agree with the *Saturday Review* of Dec. 24, 1870, that the true gestour must "shut his eyes to the possible danger of prolixity", but about an eighth of the reviews from 1867 to 1900 expressed the wish that Morris had kept his eyes open. It is interesting that some of the critics who praised the realism Morris achieved by truthful rendering of detail nonetheless felt that certain poems or portions of poems would have benefitted by compression. Swinburne, for instance, states in his review of *Jason* that diffusion is the nature of romance and we should not blame the "length and fulness of so fair a river" but advises the author that "something of a barrier or dam may serve to concentrate and condense the next". Similarly, the reviewer of *Blackwood's* (July, 1869) says that Morris heightens the interest in *Jason* "by elaborating each particular circumstance so as to give it its full picturesque effect", yet thinks that the description of the return trip of the Argonauts should be abridged. The *Times* of Oct. 10, 1868, comes closest to the position of the critics who had complained of *Guenevere's* excessive detail; in *The Earthly Paradise*, according to the reviewer, "the elaboration of the landscape deprives the figures of their proper significance". Even less kind is the *Quarterly Review* article (January, 1872) which complains that Morris has an "incurable habit of gossiping".

Part of the reason for such complaints about Morris's diffuseness was probably the sheer bulk of his achievement: *Jason* is about ten thousand lines and *The Earthly Paradise* about forty thousand lines—longer than the *Faerie Queene*. Some critics felt that no poet could write so much without carelessness; and although it is not true that Morris did not revise—May Morris points out his painstaking revisions of "The Proud King" and "The Watching of the Falcon"—it is true that he would often simply cast aside an unsatisfactory draft and write another completely different, as he did with the Prologue.[20] Moreover, there were some long passages which he never altered from the first draft, and his rapid manner of work could scarcely avoid a certain amount of diffuseness.

The comparison of Morris with Chaucer as story-teller and descriptive artist was predominantly favorable, as the examination up to this point has shown, but Morris did not fare so well in regard to four other points of comparison: characterization, dramatic power, antiquarianism, and tone. Of eighteen reviews which compared Morris's characterization with that of Chaucer, more than two-thirds, although their tenor was favorable to Morris on the whole, expressed the opinion that Morris's characters generally lacked the flesh-and-blood reality of Chaucer's characters; and seven out of ten reviews which made no mention of Chaucer's characterization criticized Morris for weak delineation of character. A few of Morris's characters were quite often singled out for praise or blame: Medea was the most popular, followed by Gudrun, Bellerophon and Kiartan; and Jason, along with other "unheroic heroes", was unpopular.

But blanket statements of praise or blame were common. John Skelton (*Fraser's*, February, 1869) extols Morris's "soaring imagination not only for incident but for characterization". And Harry Buxton Forman, in *Our Living Poets* (1871), says that Morris's "men and women *are* men and women: they love with the passion of adult and healthy persons, and not with the rose-colour sentimentality of boys and girls, or the pallid and *blasé* ferocity of jaded roués".[21] Much more frequent, however, were blanket comments of disapproval like the following: *Blackwood's* (July, 1869) states that the personages in *Jason* and *The Earthly Paradise* are interesting for "what they do, not what they are". Not even this much is granted by the *Quarterly Review* (January, 1872), which asserts that the characters in *The Earthly Paradise* are more like the colorless ones in Boccaccio's *Decameron* than those in the *Canterbury Tales*; the reader is never interested in their actions as he is in the quarrel between the Friar and the Summoner. But the reviewer's illustration betrays his limited understanding of both poets, for the Friar's argument with the Summoner is merely an interesting part of the framework of the *Canterbury Tales;* the critics were right in thinking that most of Morris's characters were not well-developed (the exceptions I noted earlier in the chapter), but neither were those of Chaucer in the individual tales. Chaucer's really memorable characters are those who tell the tales rather than those who appear in them.

Several defenders of Morris admitted that his characters were not real enough to arouse strong interest but adjudged this to be in keeping with the author's plan; that is, they accepted the Apology as an accurate indication that Morris's intention was simply to provide his readers with restful entertainment by

> Telling a tale not too importunate
> To those who in the sleepy region stay,
> Lulled by the singer of an empty day.

Typical of this view is the statement of the *Spectator* review of Part III (March 12, 1870) that, in keeping with Morris's intention to take the reader out of himself and allow him to remain a detached spectator, the characters are "incapable of exciting strong sympathy". That the reviewer has wilfully allowed himself to be led astray by too much reliance on the Apology seems obvious, for, shortly after making the above statement, he acknowledges that "The Death of Paris" contains more "fire and passion than usual" and "The Lovers of Gudrun" shows "powers of which the author's former work had given no sign", with tragic passages that compare favorably with Aeschylean drama.

Roughly the same division occurred among critics concerning Morris's dramatic power—an element which is closely connected with characterization. Those who found Morris's characters less lifelike than Chaucer's also considered the later poet's work to be lacking in the dramatic intensity which Chaucer achieved—with, on the whole, the same amount of accuracy: neither Chaucer nor Morris shows dramatic power in most of his tales, for dramatic intensity can occur only in connection with well-developed characters, as I believe. It was usually in talking about these two qualities that critics made the familiar comparison of Morris's poetry with tapestry, as well as the even more frequent analogy with dreams—after all, did not Morris say he was a "dreamer of dreams"? That some of the tales are dreamlike is undeniable, but quite a few critics insisted on pasting the label on all of them. The statement of Arthur Symons in the *Saturday Review* of Oct. 10, 1896, exemplifies this viewpoint; Symons says that Morris was content to be a dreamer of dreams, compares his verse to tapestry and dreams, and serenely pontificates:

> To read . . . "The Earthly Paradise," or "The Life and Death of Jason," is like taking opium. One abandons oneself to it, and is borne on clouds as in a gondola of the air. . . . There is not even enough sharpness of interest, or novelty in the progression, to jar one on the way. The only danger is that weariness which comes of over-much repose.

Several writers, like G. A. Simcox, went through some interesting mental contortions to make the dream-label stick. In his review of Part III (*Academy*, Feb. 12, 1870), Simcox admits that the new volume contains less "naive adventure and blithe description" and more "psychological analysis" than Parts I and II, but maintains that "we never cross the invisible line which divides the poetry of dream from the poetry of action". The intensity of Oenone's passion in "The Death of Paris" equals that of Dido but, according to Simcox, "it is far more unearthly", and Morris maintains "repose" even in "The Lovers of Gudrun" by use of the "habitual reticence and measured speech of the North". If Kiartan had the eloquence of Achilles in bewailing his wrong, "Gudrun" would match the *Iliad* as "a poem of purely human interest".

From the evidence, it is hard to escape agreeing with Annie MacDonnell (*Bookman*, September, 1896) that the catchphrase "idle singer of an empty day" probably did more harm than good to Morris's reputation. If, as indicated earlier, some reviewers welcomed *The Earthly Paradise* for the "cultured repose" which they thought Morris promised them, more were very likely prevented by the Apology from taking as seriously as they deserved some of the truly dramatic poems, such as "The Lovers of Gudrun"—and, in retrospect, *Jason*—or the fine psychological studies, such as "The Death of Paris" and "The Story of Rhodope".

Similarly, the reviewers who agreed with Morris that it was indeed an "empty day" and thought the poet did well to help them forget it were offset by those who belabored Morris for neglecting his own time and taking refuge in the past. About a fourth of the critics who compared Morris with Chaucer expressed regret that Morris was concerned with the past, whereas Chaucer had been interested in his own age; and the complaint of antiquarianism was echoed by several who did not make the comparison. Some defenders of Morris said that, since his poems did not partake of the transiency of contemporary affairs, they were more likely to last; and aesthetic critics, such as Pater, Saintsbury, and Lang, considered Morris's medievalism as the way to one of the "Paradises of Art", as I mentioned in Chapter Two. But too common were statements like that of the *Athenaeum* review of Part IV (Dec. 7, 1870), in which the writer says that Chaucer wrote of the things of his time in the language of his time, but Morris is "essentially archaic". And "why is this 'an empty day'?" the reviewer belligerently asks. "Has love, has courage, fled the earth since the disuse of mediaeval garments?" But he expresses hope that, since Morris is still a young man, he may live to repent.

This insistence that Chaucer was concerned with his own day may seem curious in view of the fact that a good part of his poetry was, like Morris's, a retelling of old tales. But Chaucer never for long allows the reader to forget that life is a pilgrimage, and it is probably the lack of such a moralistic thread in Morris's poems which prompted the disapproval of the reviewers rather than the failure to use modern subjects. If one tells an old story in such a way as to teach a useful lesson or give inspiration, as Tennyson and Browning were doing, he is, after all, more concerned with his own day than with the past. This view gains support from my earlier citations of those reviewers who welcomed Morris's poems as an escape from worldly cares but acknowledged that the noblest poetry is that which "arms us for the fight" and of those who explicitly urged Morris to assume the role of teacher.

The element in Morris's poems for which he suffered the most in the comparison with Chaucer was his fatalistic tone. A full fifth of all the commentators from 1867 to 1900 felt that the "ominous knell of death" marred the beauty of *The Earthly Paradise* and, to a lesser extent, *Jason.* At first the complaint was only a murmur; for instance, *Blackwood's* (July, 1869), at the end of an article which is almost completely laudatory of both books, expresses wonder at the melancholy of Morris, so different from Chaucer: "Why has this gift of cheerfulness been denied to the inheritor of so many of his endowments?" After the publication of Parts III and IV, the cry increased, both in numbers and intensity. The *New Monthly Magazine* (September, 1871) calls Chaucer and Morris "L'Allegro" and "Il Penseroso" because of Chaucer's good spirits and Morris's "irrepressible note of sadness". "Not a charming scene is visited, or an hour of perfect delight passed . . . without the intruding reflection that death ends it all, and it comes speedily." And the *Edinburgh Review* (January, 1871), with even more bitterness, uses the graphic illustration which quite a few later critics echoed:

> If it be hard to say whether the music of Mr. Morris's song carries with it more of pleasure than of pain, the pleasure must at the least be that of men who sit at the banquet-table in the

presence of the veiled skeleton.... That "the idle singer of an empty day" ... has given us melodies of exquisite sweetness, it would be mere ingratitude to deny; but the music of this Earthly Paradise is mournful because it is so earthly.... the language of the poet throughout is not only that of resignation to a doom of absolute extinction after a short sojourn here, but of the philosophy which makes this extinction the one justification of merriment.

Again, it seems strange that the reviewers thought Chaucer was completely cheerful, for, although the framework of the *Canterbury Tales* and the fabliaux could be called cheerful, there are quite a number of tales in which the shortness of life is lamented—as, for example, the "Knight's Tale", when Arcite complains,

"What is this world? what asketh man to have?
Now with his love, now in his colde grave
Allone, withouten any compaignye!" (2777-79) ·

But a Christian overtone is audible throughout Chaucer's work, and it is the absence of this in Morris that really bothered the reviewers more than his reminding them of "quick-coming death". As the *Spectator* of Nov. 5, 1898, observes, "It is not the frequent allusions to death amidst the loveliest scenes in the Earthly Paradise that lessens their charm, but the belief so often expressed or implied that there is no sure hope of anything beyond death." Several reviewers were so disturbed by Morris's fatalistic tone that they even approved of his becoming a Socialist poet, although they disapproved of Socialist ideology. For example, Edward Dowden, in the *Fortnightly Review* of June, 1887, admits that Morris's didactic verse cannot compare with his earlier work but rejoices that Morris is now a "singer of hope" in the London streets: "Better, far better, *Chants for Socialists* with faith, however inadequate for the wants of the soul, and hope and charity, than the *Earthly Paradise* with all of life a melancholy dream."

The comparatively few defenders of Morris's fatalism (only a third as numerous as the attackers) usually offered the argument that, although it was true that the poems evinced little of the "better hope", this was simply due to the poet's artistic integrity: in both books he put himself mentally into the epoch of the stories, and in *The Earthly Paradise* he had to assume the character of his narrators, plus maintaining the unity of the theme. As Aymer Vallance says in his biography of Morris (1897), to have omitted the occasional sounding of the *carpe diem* theme would have been to abandon the thread of the work.[22] But several critics found the fatalistic tone to be a source of strength in Morris's work. Harry Buxton Forman, in *Our Living Poets* (1871), says, "There is no trace here of unhealthy revolt against circumstance and law; and although we may learn lessons to struggle after attainable good and away from avoidable evil, we are made to feel at the same time the beauty and strength of manly submission to the inevitable."[23] And Walter Pater, in the *Westminster Review* (October, 1868), thinks that the awareness of death in the poems quickens the sense of beauty: he uses the theme as the starting-point for his famous discourse on the necessity of burning with a "hard gem-like flame".

Most reviewers did not mention any influence on *Jason* and *The Earthly Paradise* besides that of Chaucer (except insofar as they considered the sources of the tales to be influences), but a few of them pointed to Homer, Keats, Spenser, and the Icelandic Sagas as influences. The Homeric influence, usually discussed in relation to *Jason*, was most often seen in the catalogue of heroes, the use of certain habitual epithets and the "Homeric minuteness" with which the poet attended to the physical wants of the heroes. Morris called Keats one of his masters, as I have said, and George Ford states that there are clear traces of Keatsian influence on *Jason* and *The Earthly Paradise* in the manner of versification, tone, and narrative method;[24] but strangely enough, only a handful of reviewers mentioned Keats, and their comment was usually confined to remarking that Morris's enjambment was like that in *Endymion*. Spenser was regarded as an influence by a half-dozen critics who found a similarity between the two poets in archaism, lengthiness, and pageant-like effect. And several reviewers made note of the Icelandic influence which was evident in "The Fostering of Aslaug" and "The Lovers of Gudrun", but most obvious in the latter.

Despite the fact that *Jason* and *The Earthly Paradise* were based on old tales and despite the widespread recognition of the Chaucerian influence, a large majority of the critics considered the works to be basically original. The complaint that Morris was an imitative, "literary" poet was aired occasionally—usually by the same reviewers who criticized him for being out of tune with the time. But most critics would have agreed with Amy Sharp and Thomas Bayne. In *Victorian Poets* (1891), Miss Sharp says:

> Morris does not invent either his forms or the groundwork of his tales; but taking the old verse or the old legend, he re-animates it, refines away what was coarse in its primitive structure, supplies deficiencies whether in motive or symmetry, breathes new vigour and sweetness into its life, and clothing all with delicate grace and beauty, produces a whole as original in workmanship as it is beautiful in effect.[25]

And Bayne acknowledges, in the *St. James Magazine* of January, 1878, that there are various Chaucerian elements in Morris's work, but maintains that the disciple is entirely capable of speaking for himself: "He goes to Nature as well as to Chaucer, and he has a command over rhythm and melody which he owes to nobody."

The great majority of critics who mentioned Morris's diction and prosody in *Jason* and *The Earthly Paradise* found them both much improved since *Guenevere*, but some of the complaints outlined in the preceding chapter were once more aired. The objections to his use of archaisms were pretty well balanced by commendations of the "pure Saxon English" of his poems. But even those who praised Morris's diction often mildly objected to his overuse of favorite epithets, such as "wan" water, "tumbling" sea, and "slim" maidens.

Regarding Morris's prosody, in addition to the discussion of his use of Chaucerian metres, there was an occasional objection to loose rhymes and faulty scanning, but most reviewers found Morris's style to be very smooth and melodious. Yet herein lay the seed of what became a persistent complaint: because of the very smoothness of the style, it came to be considered monotonous by about a fifth of the commentators. No doubt a contributing factor, as in the complaint against diffuseness, was the great quantity of verse presented to the public in a three-year span. This conclusion is supported by the fact that the charge of "sweet monotony" was very rare until the issuance of Part III. Thus, the *London Quarterly Review* of January, 1869, praises the "gracious fluency" and "luscious sweetness" of both *Jason* and *The Earthly Paradise* (Volume I), but *Blackwood's* (May, 1870) talks of the "Full, sweet monotony of the verse" in Part III. Thereafter, the objection became one of the most common lodged against the two books. Even Swinburne expresses dissatisfaction on this score after reading Part III: in a letter to Rossetti on Dec. 10, 1869, he says that Morris's Muse, "like Homer's Trojan women ... drags her robes as she walks; I really think a Muse (when she is neither resting nor flying) ought to tighten her girdle, tuck up her skirts, and step out."[26] And Browning, perhaps fatigued by the absence of an inspiriting tone as much as by the monotony of the verse, writes to Isabella Blagden on Jan. 19, 1870, "Morris is sweet, pictorial, clever always—but a weariness to me by this time."[27]

My belief that Morris's voluminous production was in a measure responsible for the charge of "sweet monotony" is given further support by the fact that the charge was usually made by the same critics who objected to Morris's diffuseness, and by the further fact that the defence against this charge by many of Morris's admirers was that, after all, *The Earthly Paradise* was not intended to be read through at a sitting; it should be read at leisure in instalments, when one had an idle afternoon to kill. Too few were those who would agree with Saintsbury that one must not be a stop-watch critic to do Morris justice,[28] or with Forman that "to whatever length his works may run", they are "always distinctly poetry."[29]

I said at the beginning of this discussion that *Jason* and *The Earthly Paradise* were greeted by the critics with thunderous applause at their birth and completed the century at a point slightly lower in critical estimation but still remarkably high. This was true of the overall tone of the reviews, but the intervening examination has shown that this critical approval was extended along with a good number of qualifications. Oscar Maurer says the popularity of *Jason* and *The Earthly Paradise* was due mainly to their "escape" value, both as an actual escape from contemporary social and religious difficulties and as an artistic escape from the analytical and problem-haunted poetry of the time.[30] Though Maurer's viewpoint is not comprehensive enough, I think it expresses a large part of the truth: it accounts not only for those critics who wanted "cultured repose", but also for those who admired the absence of didacticism and the simple concern for Beauty in Morris's poetry, as well as for those who appreciated Morris's clear, objective narrative technique. There were other qualities in Morris, however, which aroused the admiration of the critics: most notably the pictorial quality and "fidelity to nature" of his descriptions, but also the smooth melody of his verse. On the other hand, Morris received a good deal of criticism for his refusal to treat the questions of the day, his melancholy tone, the weakness of his characterization, his lack of dramatic intensity, the diffuseness resulting from his attention to detail, and the "sweet monotony" of his verse. If one concludes from this examination that the critics were impossibly demanding, one must add that their willingness to point out at such length what they considered to be weaknesses was a tribute to the tremendous impression which *Jason* and *The Earthly Paradise* must have made upon them.

NOTES TO CHAPTER THREE

[1] Mackail, *Life of William Morris*, I, 138-61 *passim*.
[2] *Collected Works*, I, xix. The Tristram story, already treated by Arnold, was later to be handled by Swinburne, Tennyson, Hardy—and even E. A. Robinson in the United States.
[3] Mackail, I, 166-67.
[4] *Ibid.*, I, 178.
[5] *Collected Works*, V, xxvii.
[6] *Works of Geoffrey Chaucer*, ed. F. N. Robinson, second edition (Cambridge, Mass., 1957), p. 265.
[7] Graham Hough, *The Last Romantics* (London, 1949), pp. 123, 125.
[8] In the past fifty years, Chaucer's influence on Morris has been hardly touched upon, except for an occasional and usually brief reference in essays dealing with other aspects of Morris's work.
[9] *Collected Works*, II, xiv.
[10] Vaughan, *Bibliographies*, p. 7; also Forman, *Books of William Morris*, pp. 45-48.
[11] Alfred McKinley Terhune, *The Life of Edward Fitzgerald* (New Haven, 1947), p. 128.
[12] Edwin Mallard Everett, *The Party of Humanity: The Fortnightly Review and its Contributors, 1865-1874* (Chapel Hill, 1939), p. 80.
[13] Diderik Roll-Hansen, *The Academy, 1869-1879* (Copenhagen, 1957), p. 16.
[14] Oscar Wilde, *Complete Works,* ed. Robert Ross (Boston, 1908), X, 257.
[15] *The Earthly Paradise* (London, 1907), p. 65.
[16] *The George Eliot Letters*, ed. Gordon S. Haight (New Haven, 1955), IV, 451.
[17] George Saintsbury, *Corrected Impressions*, p. 190. Keats' *Lamia* may have served Morris in part for a model.
[18] *Collected Works*, XXII, xxxii.
[19] *Earthly Paradise* (1907), p. 102.
[20] May Morris, *William Morris, Artist, Writer, Socialist*, I, 404-11.
[21] Forman, *Our Living Poets* (London, 1871), p. 426.
[22] Aymer Vallance, *William Morris: His Art, His Writings, and His Public Life* (London, 1897), p. 177.

[23] Forman, *Our Living Poets*, p. 381.
[24] George Ford, *Keats and the Victorians* (New Haven, 1944), p. 156. Clarice Short, in "William Morris and Keats", *PMLA*, LIX (1944), 513-23, finds some close parallels in imagery between the two poets.
[25] Amy Sharp, *Victorian Poets* (London, 1891), p. 175.
[26] *Swinburne Letters*, ed. Cecil Lang (New Haven, 1959), II, 68.
[27] *Dearest Isa: Robert Browning's Letters to Isabella Blagden*, ed. Edward C. McAleer (Austin, Texas, 1951), pp. 328-29.
[28] Saintsbury, p. 189.
[29] Forman, *Our Living Poets*, p. 380.
[30] Oscar Maurer, Jr., "William Morris and the Poetry of Escape", *Nineteenth-Century Studies*, p. 273. It is worth noting also that Fitzgerald's *Rubáiyát* (1859), after an almost total neglect at its birth, was becoming very popular when *The Earthly Paradise* was published (Alfred McKinley Terhune, *The Life of Edward Fitzgerald*, New Haven, 1947, pp. 206-10). Although one is lyric and the other narrative poetry, the books are very similar in their emphasis on the importance of forgetting the troubles of the world and seizing beauty while life lasts.

4. THE BARD OF THE NORTH

It was *Sigurd the Volsung* (1877) which earned for Morris the title of "Bard of the North", but some reviewers thought they recognized a Norse influence in the tour de force issued four years earlier: *Love is Enough*. In the fall of 1868, Morris had begun studying the Icelandic language and literature with Eiríkr Magnússon, and the two men had collaborated on the translations of "Gunnlaug-Wormtongue" (*Fortnightly Review*, January, 1869), *Grettir the Strong* (1869), the *Völsunga Saga* (1870), and "Frithiof the Bold" (*Dark Blue*, March and April, 1871).[1] "Gunnlaug" and "Frithiof" were included in *Three Northern Love Stories* (1875), along with "Viglund the Fair" and three short tales.[2]

These translations, in addition to the fact that Morris had based "The Fostering of Aslaug" and "The Lovers of Gudrun" on Icelandic sources, led the critics to expect further influence from the North on his original poetry. Thus, when *Love is Enough* appeared in November, 1872,[3] cast in a form radically different from that of Morris's earlier work, though none of the reviewers apparently knew the source of the story, several of them conjectured that it was of Icelandic origin, while the rest remained silent on the topic; and half of them considered the model of the anapestic alliterative verse to have been the metre of the Elder Edda, from which Morris had translated some songs and appended them to the *Völsunga Saga*. But the principal verse-form of *Love is Enough* comes closer to the Middle-English alliterative measure, as the rest of the critics recognized, and since Morris cast the poem in the form of a medieval morality, there is little doubt that Mackail is correct in stating that he took the model of his verse from the same tradition.[4]

What led Morris to experiment with the morality form and alliterative measure is open to conjecture; perhaps the verse of the

Elder Edda stimulated his interest in the English development of a similar form, or perhaps, in his restless searching for something different to turn his hand to, he simply went back to the period which had furnished the material for his first book, *Guenevere*.

In looking for source-material, Morris may have been influenced by his Welsh background. *Love is Enough* is based, according to May Morris, on the old Welsh legend of "Maxen Wledig, Emperor of Rome, as given in the *Mabinogion*". Except for the root idea of the dream of a fair maiden in a distant land, however, the modern poem bears little resemblance to the Welsh tale. Maxen (the Maximus who was made emperor by his army during Gratian's reign) journeys in a dream to the fairest island in the world, where he finds a beautiful princess; after interpretation of the dream by his advisors, he proceeds to Britain, where he finds and marries the princess. Following a seven-year stay in England, Maxen returns to claim his empire, which he accomplishes at the cost of much bloodshed.[5] But in Morris's poem, King Pharamond sets out with his foster-father, Oliver, to find his dream-lover and eventually discovers her in humble surroundings; returning to his realm, he finds his throne occupied by Theobald, but declines Oliver's suggestion that he reclaim his kingdom, for that would mean slaying a good number of his own people; "Love is enough", he decides, and he goes back to his dream-maiden.

According to Mackail, Morris took more pains with *Love is Enough* than with any other poem of similar length. He must have begun working on it sometime in 1871, for Mackail quotes a letter of Oct. 2, 1871, from Rossetti to William Bell Scott:

> Morris has set to work with a will on a sort of masque called "Love is Enough".... The poem is, I think, at a higher point of execution perhaps than anything that he has done, having a passionate lyrical quality such as one found in his earliest work, and of course much more mature balance in carrying out. It will be a very fine work.

The first draft was finished by the end of the year but underwent a good deal of revision before publication.[6] Consequently, Rossetti's opinion of the quality of execution was justified: the versification of *Love is Enough* is probably the most polished to be found in Morris's poetry, and the complex structure is skilfully executed. Morris uses the frame-within-a-frame technique: the main story is enacted before the newly-married emperor and empress and the townspeople, and there are three sets of lovers besides the enacted ones of the morality: the peasants Giles and Joan, the emperor and empress, and the players who portray Pharamond and Azalais. Giles and Joan speak in octosyllabic couplets, the emperor and empress first use decasyllabic triplets with refrain but later adopt the heroic couplets which the figure of Love uses, and the body of the morality is written in a predominantly anapestic alliterative measure.

Love is Enough was the least popular of all of Morris's major poetic works. Even more than *Guenevere*, it was—and remained—caviar to the general public, and after the laudatory first reviews the same was true of critical circles. According to Harry Buxton Forman, the 1500 copies of the first edition lasted through what was called the third edition in 1889,[7] and this is probably correct, for Vaughan's bibliography shows no reissue of the book after the first edition until its inclusion in the *Poetical Works* (1896).[8]

Probably because of the great fame which Morris had gained from *Jason* and *The Earthly Paradise*, *Love is Enough* received at its birth a more generous welcome from the critics than had been accorded to *Guenevere*: not only was it recognized by a larger number of reviews in the literary journals (eight from 1872 to 1874), but the tenor of the reviews was largely favorable. After 1874, however, the book was virtually ignored by literary critics who discussed Morris's work: from 1875 to 1895, only about a half-dozen critical articles mentioned *Love*, and even during the spate of Morris criticism which followed his death, less than a third of the articles contained any reference to the book. Moreover, almost all the notices that *Love* received during the entire last quarter of the century were merely passing references—usually a line or two, very rarely more than a paragraph. Necessarily, then, the following discussion of the critical reception of *Love is Enough* will draw largely on the first eight reviews, although several conclusions will be based on the later commentary.

The early reviewers liked *Love is Enough* mainly for three reasons: the variety and technical excellence of its versification—particularly the revival of the Middle-English alliterative measure; its didactic purpose; and its pictorial quality. The weaknesses they pointed to most often were two: its obscurity and its deficiency in human interest—that is, they considered the characterization weak and the action negligible; it was, as some reviewers had said of *The Earthly Paradise*, too "dreamlike".

It is probably significant of the general feeling of this weakness in content that most of the reviewers gave more space to the prosody of the poem than to its other features. They praised the octosyllabic couplets of the dialogues between Giles and Joan and the heroic couplets used by Love and the emperor and empress—without the familiar complaint about loose rhymes lodged against Morris's earlier books; but they talked most about Morris's "bold innovation" in using the alliterative measure, both in the rhymed lyrical passages of "Music" and in the body of the morality. A majority of the critics, including those writing after 1874, agreed that the alliterative measure had been so long in disuse that its revival in the nineteenth century had the force of invention, and Morris had enlarged the limits of modern English verse by using it.

The fullest discussion of this topic is that of the *Athenaeum* of Nov. 23, 1872. Asserting that the alliterative measure is perhaps the only purely national verse-form, the reviewer states that Morris has improved on the verse of *Piers Plowman*. Not only does his fusion of the two short lines into one give more freedom in the use of alliteration, but by his "admirable innovation" of starting a new alliterative wave before the preceding one has subsided, Morris "produces an inexpressibly rich and far-reaching echo of sounds. By such means the sense is thrown into vivid relief. We not merely realize a scene, or an image, by means of a mental effort, but are brought into an immediate sensuous contact with it."

Several reviewers, while praising the finish of Morris's alliterative verse, found a certain tendency to monotony in the form. The *Spectator* of Jan. 11, 1873, says, "Mr. Morris certainly contrives to make the versification less monotonous than one would expect, but still there is a monotony of cadence which leaves an echo in the mind quite irrespective of the words." Much more critical is the comment of Henry Hewlett, in the *Contemporary Review* (December, 1874), that the "sing-song monotony of the dactylic measure" and the "cloying alliteration" produce a total effect of weakness. On the other hand, a couple of critics admitted the tendency to monotony, but thought that Morris had circumvented this tendency by, in the words of the *London Quarterly Review* (April, 1873), making the scenes "many and short" and the Music "of such a character and quality as to harmonise perfectly with the scenes while in strong contrast with them."

A source of monotony, however, which some reviewers had found in Morris's earlier works—diffusion of detail—was absent from *Love is Enough*, according to the critics; half of the first reviews made no mention of this defect, and the other half called attention to the concentration evident in the poem. For instance, Sidney Colvin, in the *Fortnightly Review* (Jan. 1, 1873), notes that Morris's verse is more concentrated than usual, and George Fraser, in *Dark Blue* (January, 1873), points to the "most masterly thirty lines" in which Oliver reminds Pharamond of the troubles they have endured during the past three years, as an answer to "those who have been wont to accuse Mr. Morris of garrulity".

One quality of *Love is Enough* which most of the early, and even some of the later, critics agreed upon was the lyrical beauty of the interspersed songs labeled "Music". The *Athenaeum* calls them "the crowning beauties of the poem", and quite a few other critics were of similar opinion—some, like the *Spectator* writer, considered them superior to the Songs of the Months in *The Earthly Paradise*.

The didactic purpose of *Love is Enough* met with unanimous approval by the first reviews. The critics were delighted not only because Morris was apparently abandoning the garment of the simple story-teller for that of the teacher, but because they approved of the lesson. George Fraser, it is true, expresses the wish that the lesson were a higher one: he agrees with Morris that love is enough for earthly happiness, without wealth, power, or fame, but is sorry "that here, in this exquisitely beautiful work, he has left this earthly Love supreme, has made him no servant of an Almighty Master". But the other reviewers gave unqualified approval to the theme of the morality, and some were especially pleased to find the melancholy tone of the two preceding books replaced by a message of hope. Thus, G. A. Simcox, in the *Academy* of Dec. 15, 1872, comments that the book "is written throughout with an intensity and seriousness which many readers will be inclined to contrast favourably with the half querulous half indolent *insouciance* which runs through much of the *Earthly Paradise*"; and Henry Hewlett, though his opinion of the book is largely unfavorable, finds reason in *Love is Enough* to hope that Morris will eventually "attain spiritual confidence", since the morality teaches that love is "a certain solace for this world, and even, as one passage seems to hint, a ground of hope for another".

As had been the case with *Jason* and *The Earthly Paradise*, the critics were generous in their praise of the pictorial art in *Love is Enough*. Quite typical is Fraser's remark that the book contains many "most exquisite pictures throughout, in the old manner which we love so well", and equally typical are his examples. He draws special attention to the speech of Azalais to the sleeping Pharamond as she describes the scenes he will see when he awakens in her homestead:

> How the rose-boughs hang in o'er the little loft window,
> And the blue bowl with roses is close to thine hand,
> And over thy bed is the quilt sown with lilies,
> And the loft is hung round with the green Southland hangings,

and the description of the peasants' home in Joan's closing speech:

> Yea, full fain would I rest thereby,
> And watch the flickering martins fly,
> About the long eave-bottles red
> And the clouds lessening overhead:
> E'en now meseems the cows are come
> Unto the gray gates of our home,
> And low to hear the milking pail:
> The peacock spreads abroad his tail
> Against the sun. . . .

Of the latter excerpt, Fraser says, "Never have we read in poetry so sweet a rustic scene as this. Full of movement, and sound, and colour, we have Joan's homestead clearly in our eyes." These two passages, along with several descriptions of Azalais in Pharamond's account of his dreams to Oliver, were the most commonly cited examples of the "exquisite pictures" in *Love is Enough*, and in fact there are few others to cite. It seems evident that, because of Morris's great reputation for having shown this quality in his earlier work, the reviewers were straining to find proof of the same skill in his latest book. *Love is Enough* does not possess the abundance of pictures which was usual with Morris, for the simple reason that it is cast in dramatic, rather than narrative, form.

On the other side of the ledger, about half of the early reviewers drew attention to the obscurity of the morality. Simcox, for example, observed that the book does not carry the reader "along a swift current of adventure" as did *The Earthly Paradise*; "we have to live in the poem, not to dream of it", so that it will not be surprising if *Love is Enough* attracts fewer readers, although "those attracted will be held longer under a deeper spell". Likewise, Colvin finds the poem more puzzling than Morris's other works, partly because of the figure of Love playing the chorus and partly because some of the incidents are "a bit shadowy"; he agrees that the reader must read himself into the morality but on so doing he will find "much loveliness and singular originality". The charge of obscurity was also admitted by two of the book's most ardent admirers, Harry Buxton Forman and Coventry Patmore, who told Forman he considered *Love is Enough* to be Morris's masterpiece.[9] In *The Books of William Morris Described* (1897) Forman calls the book "one of the most noteworthy poems of the third quarter of the century" but acknowledges that it is "above the heads of the large public to which *The Earthly Paradise* appeals."[10] And Patmore, in a letter to an unidentified correspondent, states that *Love is Enough* has "a most lofty and delicate atmosphere of mystic tenderness and joy. I don't know that a poem can have higher praise. But it is one of those things which, as Lord Dundreary says, 'No fellow can be expected to understand.'"[11]

A more serious charge against *Love is Enough*, in the minds of half of the early reviewers, was its deficiency in human interest. The *Athenaeum* writer says that, on reading "this dream within a dream", he experienced "exquisite enjoyment" mixed with a "shade of regret" that Morris did not devote his rare mastery of "a truly magnificent form of versification" to a nobler subject, such as the Arthurian legend, which the poet had already treated in fragmentary form in *Guenevere*; for Pharamond is only a "vague shadowy king, whose deeds impress us with a sense of unreality akin to his dreams". And Hewlett thinks that Pharamond is unheroic, a character who "may excite sympathy but not admiration", Azalais is "a dimly-defined conception", and Oliver is the only "natural character"; of the action, Hewlett states that it is non-existent. These judgments were seconded by several later critics; for instance, Andrew Lang (*Contemporary Review*, August, 1882) dismisses *Love is Enough* as a "brief decorative poem" which is "somewhat visionary and vague"; and Arthur Symons (*Saturday Review*, Oct. 10, 1896) includes the poem with *Jason* and *The Earthly Paradise* as books which convey the impression of an opium dream.

After 1874, as I noted earlier, critical attention to *Love is Enough* declined drastically. In the later brief references to it, the most common judgment expressed, even by critics who praised the poem, was that it was merely an interesting experiment. A good example of this view is Thomas Bayne's comment (*St. James Magazine*, January, 1878) that *Love* is a "very pretty and attractive Morality" with some beautiful lyrical passages, but that it is, after all, a mere experiment—"such, indeed, as to have made the fortune of another, but not calculated to enhance the fame that rested on works like 'The Life and Death of Jason' and 'Earthly Paradise'". Forman's high estimate of the work stood almost alone among the later commentaries; and for the majority of later critics, Morris might never have written *Love is Enough*. Apparently, like George Meredith, after looking at the book, they "looked away", considering the one look sufficient.[12]

Thus, in contrast with *Guenevere*, which started at an undeservedly low level in critical estimation but eventually achieved wide recognition, *Love is Enough*, though not copiously reviewed, began at an undeservedly high level in the judgment of the reviewers but descended to near-oblivion. The descent was probably inevitable, for *Love* is not only the slightest of Morris's five major poetic works in bulk—only a third the length of *Jason*—but it also produces the slightest impact. After admiring the finish of the versification and the beauty of some of the lyrical passages, one can hardly fail to agree with those critics who found the poem lacking in action and characterization. The weakness does not necessarily stem from Morris's use of dramatic instead of narrative form, for "Sir Peter Harpdon's End" is also written as a drama, but the characters are real, the action exciting. The morality *is* dreamlike, probably because Morris intended it so, but it cannot rank with his four other major works.

The second major poem which Morris produced during what the critics regarded as his "Northern" period is as full of action as *Love* is void of it. *Sigurd the Volsung* represents, I believe, the summit of Morris's poetic achievement. According to May Morris, the poet himself held this opinion of it: "All his Icelandic study and travel, all his feeling for the North, led up to this, and his satisfaction with it did not waver or change to the last."[13] Certainly Morris considered the root story among the noblest in history, for the preface to the *Völsunga Saga* states, "This is the Great Story of the North, which should be to all our race what the Tale of Troy was to the Greeks",[14] and when Magnússon first suggested the legend of Sigurd to Morris as a poetic subject, the poet thought the topic "too sacred, too venerable, to be touched by a modern hand".[15]

In looking to Icelandic sources for inspiration, Morris was not strictly a pioneer; there had been an Icelandic tradition in England since the publication in 1768 of two seminal poems by Thomas Gray: "The Fatal Sisters" was a paraphrase of an eleventh-century court poem entitled the "Lay of Darts", and "The Descent of Odin" paraphrased an ancient Icelandic lay, "Balder's Doom".[16] Frank Farley notes that Gray's appended explanations were evidence of the widespread ignorance of Norse mythology.[17] Also appearing in 1768 was Thomas Percy's *Five Pieces of Runic Poetry Translated from the Islandic Language*; and two years later Percy published (under the title of *Northern Antiquities*) his translation of the source of his interest: Paul Henri Mallet's *L'introduction à l'histoire de Dannemarc* (1755).[18] The work of Gray and Percy awakened a considerable interest in Norse literature; in the next forty years, translations, imitations, or adaptations of episodes from the Eddas and sagas were produced by a score of minor poets and essayists.[19]

The first writer of importance in the nineteenth century to show more than a superficial acquaintance with Norse literature was Sir Walter Scott. Scott knew enough about the subject to write a review of William Herbert's *Poems and Translations* (*Edinburgh Review*, October, 1806) and to compose an "Abstract" of the *Eyrbyggja Saga* (1814); moreover, some of Scott's original writings give evidence of Norse influence, most notably the poem "Harold the Dauntless" (1817) and the story "The Pirate" (1821).[20]

The Twenties and Thirties saw no noteworthy literary activity with Icelandic materials, but there was already enough of a tradition to stimulate Carlyle to become an eager reader of Icelandic literature in translation and to give a lecture in May, 1840 on Norse mythology (Lecture I, *On Heroes, Hero-Worship, and the Heroic in History*).[21] The Forties provided two very influential translations: Sir George Webbe Dasent's *Prose Edda* (1842) and Samuel Laing's *Heimskringla* (1844).[22] A rash of travel books on Iceland appeared in the Fifties; probably the most influential of these was Lord Dufferin's *Letters from High Latitudes* (1857).[23] And the Sixties saw a renewal of interest in translation, with the publication of *Burnt Njal* (1861) and *Gisli the Outlaw* (1866) by Dasent, the *Saga of Viga-Glum* (1866) by

Sir Edmund Head, the *Elder Edda* by Benjamin Thorpe,[24] and *Icelandic Legends* (1864-66) by Magnússon and George E. J. Powell.[25]

With this wealth of Icelandic material available, it is not surprising that Morris became interested in it. According to Magnússon, when he met Morris, the poet was already acquainted with Dasent's *Burnt Njal* and *Gisli the Outlaw*, Thorpe's *Elder Edda*, Mallet's *Northern Antiquities* (Percy's translation), and Scott's "Abstract" of the *Eyrbyggja Saga*; and from modern travel books, Morris had learned a good deal about the geography of Iceland.[26]

Although there was, then, an appreciable Icelandic tradition, very little of it deserved the name of original literature. The only Victorian work that fits this category before that of Morris was Arnold's "Balder Dead" (1855), which was based on the *Younger Edda* in Mallet's *Northern Antiquities*.[27] As B. Ifor Evans observes, Morris "exploited Icelandic resources which, despite Gray's experiments, had remained strangely neglected".[28] And if Morris was not quite a trail-blazer, he was the first to produce an original work of real magnitude in English, based on Icelandic sources.

After amusing himself by translating the *Aeneid* (1875), Morris began working on *Sigurd* on Oct. 15, 1875, according to his own notation, and he completed it late the following year; he was not occupied by any other large projects at the time, outside of the business, so that most of his spare time for about a year was devoted to *Sigurd*—a considerable time for Morris to spend on one poem.[29] If we consider *The Earthly Paradise* to be a series of poems loosely connected by a unifying thread, *Sigurd* is Morris's longest single poem—over 10,000 lines of hexameter couplets—but the metre tends less to monotony than any other narrative verse-forms used by Morris, for it allows great variation of metric feet: iambs are freely mixed with anapests, with an occasional trochee, spondee, or dactyl thrown in. Monotony is further avoided and dramatic intensity increased by the frequent dialogue: *Sigurd* contains more than any other of Morris's long narrative poems; and in scenes of great import, Morris often achieves a heightened effect by the device of stichomythia which the Greek tragedians had used with such force. For example, in Book II, after Sigurd has given Fafnir his death-blow, they exchange the following dialogue:

"Child, child, who art thou that hast smitten? bright child, of whence is thy birth?"
"I am called the Wild-thing Glorious, and alone I wend on the earth."
"Fierce child, and who was thy father?—Thou has cleft the heart of the Foe!"
"Am I like to the sons of men-folk, that my father I should know?"
"Wert thou born of a nameless wonder? shall the lies to my death-day cling?"
"How lieth Sigurd the Volsung, and the Son of Sigmund the King?"
"O bitter father of Sigurd!—thou has cleft mine heart atwain!"
"I arose, and I wondered and wended, and I smote, and I smote not in vain."
"What master hath taught thee of murder?—Thou hast wasted Fafnir's day."
"I, Sigurd, knew and desired, and the bright sword learned the way."[30]

Sigurd is divided into four books: "Sigmund" deals with the death of Volsung and all his sons except Sigmund at the hands of Siggeir, Sigmund's revenge with the aid of his sister Signy and their incestuous offspring Sinfiotli, and Sigmund's death before his son Sigurd is born; "Regin" tells of Sigurd's birth and training by the dwarf Regin, his slaying of the serpent Fafnir and of Regin, his taking of the Hoard of Andvari, and his awaking of Brynhild on Hindfell; in "Brynhild" Sigurd goes to the land of the Niblungs, drinks a love-potion which makes him forget Brynhild and marry Gudrun, woos Brynhild for Gunnar, and is slain by Guttorm at Brynhild's instigation, after which Brynhild kills herself; and "Gudrun" relates Gudrun's marriage to Atli, her arrangement of the slaughter of the Niblungs in revenge for Sigurd's death, her burning of the Hall of Atli, and her suicide.

Whether or not Morris was disappointed at Sigurd's reception by the public, as Mackail thinks,[31] it did not sell as well as *Jason* and *The Earthly Paradise*, although it sold better than *Guenevere* or *Love is Enough*. The first edition of 2500 copies, which came out in November, 1876, was not quite exhausted at the time of the second edition in 1887,[32] and the poem was not reissued again until its publication in the *Poetical Works*.[33]

The critics were more generous than the public. Theodore Watts-Dunton, the friend and keeper of Swinburne and a staunch admirer of Morris, writes in the *Athenaeum* of Dec. 4, 1897, that *Sigurd* was neglected by the critics. His memory is certainly faulty, for, though *Sigurd* did not receive the voluminous attention accorded its two famous fore-runners, ten reviewers, writing in most of the important literary journals of the day, devoted a total of almost sixty pages to the book from December, 1876 to January, 1878. From the latter date until the close of the century, *Sigurd* was mentioned more than thirty times; true, about half of these references were quite brief, but they were usually extremely favorable, not like the curt dismissals of *Love is Enough*. A good example is E. D. A. Morehead's review of the *Odyssey* as translated by Morris; writing in the *Academy* of March 3, 1888, Morehead judges Morris's translation to be worthy of the pen that wrote *Sigurd* and *The Earthly Paradise*, and "few would desire higher praise".

Judging from the content of the reviews and not their numbers, the critical reception of *Sigurd* was more favorable than that of *Jason* and *The Earthly Paradise*. Four-fifths of the first reviews were predominantly favorable, and this proportion continued to the end of the century; this was the same percentage of approval awarded the more famous books in later criticism, though not so high as that which had greeted their birth; but more important is the fact that the critics generally found more to praise and less to blame in *Sigurd* than in the earlier works.

There was good reason for the popularity of *Sigurd* with the critics: in addition to the direct narrative style which had been widely approved in *Jason* and *The Earthly Paradise*, the poem suggested "noble grounds for the noble emotions", which was the mark of great poetry in Ruskin's opinion (*Modern Painters*, III, 1856); or as Arnold would have put it, *Sigurd* presented a great action with "high seriousness" ("Study of Poetry", 1880). Thus, whereas a good portion of the admirers of Morris's previous narrative poems thought they were excellent of their kind but not of the best kind, more than half of the reviewers of *Sigurd* regarded it as Morris's greatest work, and about three-quarters of them classed it as a true epic, which they considered the noblest kind of poetry. No longer was Morris simply an entertaining story-teller, for in *Sigurd* he had attained the exalted position of a singer of heroic actions and high tragedy.

Several reviewers persisted in wearing the blinders which they had fashioned for themselves from the Apology to *The Earthly Paradise*. Henry Morley, for instance, in the *Nineteenth Century* (November, 1877), states that Morris has once again taken for his subject an old story with pictorial incidents and "too far from modern life to stir deep emotion", so that personal interest will not interfere with the reader's enjoyment of the poet's story-telling skill.

But these few voices were drowned in the chorus of those proclaiming Morris's coronation as the bard of the North. Thus, Theodore Watts-Dunton, in the *Athenaeum* of Dec. 9, 1876, identifies Morris with Bragi, the Norse god of poetry: "Mr. Morris is the very *Frunsmidr Bragar*—the Poetry-Smith of the Northern Olympus." *Sigurd*, says Watts-Dunton, is Morris's greatest achievement because its central theme is the heroic creed of the "fighter, whose business it is to fight, to yield to no power whatsoever, whether of earth, or heaven, or hell". Likewise, Edmund Gosse, in the *Academy* of the same date, exults that Morris is no longer an "idle singer" but "the interpreter of high desires and ancient heroic hopes as fresh as the dawn of the world and as momentous". And the *London Quarterly Review* of April, 1877, also notes with satisfaction that Morris has taken up "the stern position of a poet concerned with the affairs of man's life and destinies" and finds the "distant future of the human spirit" symbolized in the "history of Sigurd Agonistes and the Fall of the Ancient Gods".

This attitude continued prevalent for the rest of the century. Watts-Dunton's opinion of *Sigurd* in the *Athenaeum* of Oct. 10, 1896, is, if anything, higher than before, for he calls it "the greatest epic of the nineteenth century". Harry Buxton Forman, in the *Illustrated London News* of the same date, rates *Sigurd* even higher: in the qualities "which derive from knowledge of life, feeling for national myth, epic action and tragic intensity combined, 'The Story of Sigurd the Volsung' ... stands among the foremost poems not only of this century, but of our literature". And the *Quarterly Review* of October, 1899, goes Forman one better and ranks *Sigurd* among "the epic poems of the world."

Equally compelling as evidence of the lofty critical estimate of *Sigurd* is the extreme rarity of serious objections. Henry Hewlett, for instance, is almost alone in doubting that the theme of *Sigurd* is noble enough for an epic poem; in *Fraser's* (July, 1877), Hewlett acknowledges that some characteristics of the Norse spirit which the poem illustrates are praiseworthy—resignation to the inevitable, trust in divine ordinances, endurance of pain, and contempt of death—but judges that the predominance of the revenge motive deprives *Sigurd* of any strong claim to interest, for modern moralists agree that "love is the noblest, revenge the meanest, of human motives". Just as rare is the complaint of Nowell Smith, in the *Fortnightly Review* of December, 1897, that *Sigurd* is pervaded by the same fatalistic tone which infected *Jason* and *The Earthly Paradise*; Smith cites the statement of Signy in Book I to prove his point:

> "Heavy and hard are the Norns; but each man his burden bears;
> And what am I to fashion the fate of the coming years?"

And in view of the fact that the sense of fate is stronger than in any of the other major poems of Morris, it may seem strange that the complaint is so rare; but Smith himself provides the answer when he refers to the occasional passages where "the yearning for the brightness and happiness of the age of gold, which is usually represented as something that has long passed away, seems to be transmuted by its own intense heat into a hope of some future state of bliss"—which makes us wonder why Smith made the accusation. The example that Smith quotes is the passage in Book II in which Regin tells Sigurd of the visit of three gods to earth:

> "And the three were the heart-wise Odin, the Father of the Slain,
> And Loki, the World's Begrudger, who maketh all labour vain,
> And Haenir, the Utter-Blameless who wrought the hope of man,
> And his heart and inmost yearnings, when first the work began;—
> —The God that was aforetime, and hereafter yet shall be,
> When the new light yet undreamed of shall shine o'er earth and sea."

This is characteristic of the note that is continually sounded throughout the book. The Volsungs not only resign themselves to fate but feel that they are helping the gods to bring about what they have decreed; it is made clear by Odin's planting the fated sword in the Branstock early in Book I and by his intermittent reappearance, as well as by the occasional statement of a character that he is helping the gods to work out their plan. As the *Quarterly Review* (October, 1899) says, *Sigurd* is "the religious epic of the North, and it is the life of the gods, and their war with evil, for and through man, which furnishes its ultimate thread—deep-hidden in the tragedy of the life of the Volsungs." Moreover, the shortness of life is not a cause for melancholy with the Volsungs; instead, it spurs them to pile up glorious deeds so that they will sit in God-home with Odin. Therefore, it is not surprising that the critics swallowed the fatalism of *Sigurd* with scarcely a murmur, whereas they had choked on that of *The Earthly Paradise*.

In contrast to the critical indictment of Morris's concern with the past in his first three books of poetry, the reviewers of *Sigurd* found its antiquarianism only a cause for approval. They praised the manner in which Morris had recreated the atmosphere of his subject. Edmund Gosse, for example, says, "In this poem, so steeped is the author in the records of the heroic past, so intimately are his sympathies connected with those of the mythical age of which he writes, that we walk with demigods to the close." And Watts-Dunton finds "no affectation" in the antiquarianism of *Sigurd*: "The poet is quite soaked in Odinism. . . . He consents to breathe the smoke with us, but it is in the atmosphere of the Golden Past that he lives. The consequence is, that the spontaneity—real and not apparent merely— of this reproduction of the temper of a bygone age is as marvellous as the spontaneity of the form in which it is embodied."[34] The prevalence of this attitude toward *Sigurd* gives additional support to my earlier contention that, when the critics objected to the use of an antique subject in a poem, it was usually because they found no edification in it.

As might be expected from the reviewers' high regard for *Sigurd* as an epic, there was widespread commendation of its characterization and dramatic intensity. Several reviewers found the poem lacking in both elements, but the vast majority thought otherwise. The critics pointed out various especially dramatic passages, such as the revenge of the Volsungs upon Siggeir and Signy's return to share the fiery death of her husband, Sigurd's slaying of Fafnir and Regin, the slaying of Sigurd and suicide of Brynhild, and the grief of Gudrun; but the passage most often cited was the massacre of the Niblungs in the Hall of Atli, with Gudrun sitting like a statue above the slaughter. This scene, says Watts-Dunton, is "two hundred lines of narrative poetry quite unsurpassed in our language—unsurpassed perhaps in any other".[35] And Thomas Bayne, in the *St. James Magazine* (January, 1878), finds in *Sigurd* "masculine vigour and robustness throughout as befits the nature of the theme" but thinks the conclusion above all, "is grandly tragic, there being in the weird silence and immobility of Gudrun an Aeschylean conception and grasp".

In considering Morris's characterization, the critics usually talked about his improvement on his originals. There was virtually no mention of influences, other than that of the Icelandic source material, and Morris's handling of that material was regarded as highly original by almost all of the reviewers. Typical is the statement of Edmund Gosse: Morris, he says, has "poured his rich and copious language into the great mould of his Icelandic model. It must not be understood from this that the poem is a translation, or in any way whatsoever undeserving in the highest sense of the praise due to imaginative originality. Merely the framework of narrative is the old time-honoured one."

Morris's originality is especially evident, as the critics recognized, in the manner in which he alters and fills out the characters of the chief personages in his sources. Signy, says the *London Quarterly Review* (April 1877), in the *Völsunga Saga*, is a "barely-sketched type of certain savage needs of semi-civilised man", but in Morris's version she has the feminine tenderness of a fully-equipped woman, and her action becomes a "much greater self-sacrifice as her nature is made more queenly". The somewhat masculine Brynhild of the saga, "with the thews and tastes of a warrior", according to the *Times* (Feb. 9, 1877), "is refined into the wise and beautiful Brynhild, shrinking and flushing under a humiliating intrigue that outraged the delicacy of her womanhood". Likewise, as Thomas Bayne points out, the Amazonian Gudrun of the saga is feminized by Morris into a clinging, faithful wife. But Morris's characterization of Sigurd received the highest encomiums. Fairly representative is the statement by the *London Quarterly Review* that Morris has taken the somewhat shadowy idea of Sigurd and his great unspeakable woe and "built him up into something thoroughly articulate and universal. He moves through the grand and stately measures of the poem a figure of light and beneficence, and yet thoroughly a man; and the unshapen woe of his life finds here a clearer utterance and a keener edge than has ever been given it before."

Part of Morris's method of making his characters sympathetic was the omission or alteration of various barbaric episodes in the Icelandic original, and this was especially gratifying to the critics. The original Signy, for instance, sends two sons, one after the other, to Sigmund with instructions to do away with them if they prove useless to him, and after testing the boys, he kills them; in *Sigurd* she sends only one son before Sinfiotli, and Sigmund sends him home instead of killing him. The character of Gudrun is likewise softened: in the saga she eats part of the serpent's heart following her marriage to Sigurd, and after the slaughter of the Niblungs she kills her children and feeds their hearts to Atli before killing him; but both of these incidents are omitted in Morris's poem. Hewlett, in his *Fraser's* article (July, 1877), expresses the tenor of critical opinion in adjudging these modifications to be evidence of the poet's "delicate sensibility".

One aspect of Morris's verse which had been much praised in reviews of his previous books—the pictorial quality—was comparatively neglected by the reviewers of *Sigurd*. Almost half of the first reviews mentioned it as one of the praiseworthy features of the book, but they did not quote examples; and the topic hardly ever arose in later commentaries. One explanation might be that, since there is a good deal more dialogue in *Sigurd* than in Morris's earlier narrative poetry, the poet devotes less space to description. But even so, *Sigurd* contains an abundance of vividly descriptive passages, both of nature and of men and their works. The probable answer is that the reviewers considered the action more important than the pictures, and so did Morris: in much of his earlier poetry, Morris appeared to delight in painting detailed pictures for their own sake, but in *Sigurd* the description is consistently subordinated to the story. Morris was obeying the dictum handed down by Arnold in the Preface to his *Poems* twenty-three years earlier—that the poet should "prefer his action to everything else; so to treat this, as to permit its inherent excellences to develop themselves, without interruption from the intrusion of his personal peculiarities".[36]

In support of this explanation, it may be noted that all the descriptions of Sigurd are consistent with his symbolic representation as a sun-god, the bringer of light—a representation which several reviewers recognized—and that even the natural descriptions reinforce this effect. For example, in Book II, when Regin and Sigurd are climbing toward the Glittering Heath, the dawn and Sigurd are strikingly visualized thus:

> And the cloudy flecks were scattered like flames on the heaven's floor,
> And all was kindled at once, and that trench of the mountains grey
> Was filled with the living light as the low sun lit the way:
> But Regin turned from the glory with blinded eyes and dazed,
> And lo, on the cloudy war-steed how another light there blazed....[37]

In contrast with the large amount of attention given to the technical aspects of *Love is Enough*, the reviewers of *Sigurd*, although most of them mentioned technique, gave relatively little space to it, which is probably a further indication of the impact which the content of the poem had upon them. The great majority of comments on this topic were favorable; complaints were much fewer than had been the case with Morris's first three books. There was no mention of faulty scanning or inexact rhymes; and in truth the versification of *Sigurd* shows more technical excellence than that of any of Morris's other major poetic works except *Love is Enough*. Several critics thought the metre tended to monotony, but they were far outnumbered by those who praised the sustained melody of the verse, and there was no complaint against "cloying sweetness" as there had been against *Jason* and *The Earthly Paradise*. Also, though a handful of reviewers criticized Morris's archaisms, a great many more thought the diction pure and appropriate, the style simple but exalted, as befitted an epic poem. For example, Watts-Dunton comments that "for purity of English, for freedom from euphuism and every kind of 'poetic diction' (so-called), it is far ahead of anything of equal length that has appeared in this century".[38] Of the style, Edmund Gosse says that it is "more exalted and less idyllic, more rapturous and less luxurious—in a word, more spirited and more virile than that of any of his earlier works", and he asserts that no "lesser genius would have succeeded in winging a level flight through so many thousand lines without sinking to the plane of common men and common thoughts".

The only objection against *Sigurd* which was urged by more than a handful of writers was one which had plagued *Jason* and more especially *The Earthly Paradise*: lengthiness. About a fifth of the reviewers said that *Sigurd* suffered from lack of compression—with less reason than ever before, as I think the brief discussion of Morris's subordination of picture to story should indicate to some extent. Some of them were doubtless influenced by Morris's prodigious energy; they simply could not understand how Morris could produce so much and refused to believe that such voluminous production could result in excellence. For instance, the *Spectator* of Feb. 3, 1877, says of Morris, "We cannot help thinking that the ease with which he writes sometimes betrays him into too great diffuseness. Three epics in little over three years, and two of such tremendous length as the *Aeneid* and *Sigurd*, are almost too much for any man who gives due attention to his work." (The third "epic" was presumably either *Love is Enough* or the translation of *Three Northern Love Stories*.) And H. H. Statham, in the *Edinburgh Review* of January, 1897, declares sententiously that a great epic cannot be written "in intervals of business"; after all, Milton spent years on *Paradise Lost* and thought twelve lines a good morning's work. Even if it were true that an epic demands full-time attention, Morris did not confine his poetic activity to non-business hours, but often thought out passages while working; "if a chap can't compose an epic poem while he's weaving tapestry", he once said, "he had better shut up, he'll never do any good at all".[39] These reviewers, of course, simply had no inkling of Morris's tremendous productive capacity, but they also were suffering under the delusion that Morris merely dashed off his poems as the spirit moved him; May Morris's documented account of the careful rewriting, revision, and cutting that went into the making of *Sigurd* would have done much to disabuse them.[40]

More justifiable was the objection of several critics against *Sigurd's* length on the ground that it was destructive of unity; they especially regarded as superfluous all of the poem preceding Sigurd's birth. G. A. Simcox, in his review of the *Völsunga Saga* (*Academy*, Aug. 13, 1870), expresses very well the sentiment of these reviewers when he says that the *Saga* is constructed on the principle of "beginning the Trojan War with Leda's Egg". But, although the story of Sigmund and Signy is not strictly necessary to the work, it looks forward to the story of *Sigurd* and gives a greater sense of the working-out of the will of Odin, which can be said to provide the larger unity of the poem.

I think this examination of the *Sigurd* commentary has shown that, although the book did not achieve the fame of *Jason* and *The Earthly*

Paradise, it was far from being neglected by the critics, and the criticism contains proportionately more approval and less disapproval than that of any of Morris's previous poetic works. Thus, in the two major poems of his "Northern" period, Morris reached both the depth and, with the forementioned qualifications, the height of his poetic reputation. *Love is Enough* impressed the first reviewers by its technical virtuosity and satisfied their desire for uplift, but had little else to commend it. Apparently, after all, love was *not* enough for the critics; they wanted some action. Moreover, Alba Warren's observation that, although the majority of early Victorian critics considered the proper end of poetry to be instruction or inspiration, they preferred to have this end reached by indirection,[41] appears to continue valid for the remainder of the century. *Love is Enough*, though not a sermon, makes its point too directly and reiterates it too often to have been really satisfactory to most critics. On the other hand, *Sigurd* provides inspiration without preaching and an exciting story which can be enjoyed for itself, told in a clear style and sprinkled with beautiful pictures. It was therefore well-equipped to satisfy both moralistic and aesthetic critics. It is significant that the aesthetic critic Arthur Symons regards *Sigurd* as "a masterpiece of sustained power" and finds no contradiction in his statement, "Now, at last, he touches the heart.... And still, more than ever, he is the poet of beauty."[42]

NOTES TO CHAPTER FOUR

[1] *Collected Works*, VII, xv, xxxiv; and X, x.
[2] Mackail, *Life of William Morris*, I, 300.
[3] C. E. Vaughan, *Bibliographies*, p. 7.
[4] Mackail, I, 285.
[5] May Morris, *William Morris*, I, 444-45.
[6] Mackail, I, 280.
[7] Harry Buxton Forman, *Books of William Morris Described* (London, 1897), p. 48.
[8] Vaughan, p. 7.
[9] Forman, p. 80.
[10] *Ibid.*, p. 7.
[11] *Memoirs and Correspondence of Coventry Patmore*, ed. Basil Champneys (London, 1900), II, 97.
[12] *Letters of George Meredith*, ed. W. M. Meredith (New York, 1912), p. 240—letter to Frederick Greenwood, Jan. 1, 1873.

[13] Collected Works, XII, xxiii.
[14] *Ibid.*, VII, 286.
[15] Eirikr Magnússon, *Cambridge Review*, Nov. 26, 1896, p. 110.
[16] *The Works of Thomas Gray*, ed. Edmund Gosse (London, 1884), I, 54, 60.
[17] Frank E. Farley, *Scandinavian Influences in the English Romantic Movement*, in *Studies and Notes in Philology and Literature* (Boston, 1903), IX, 1.
[18] *Ibid.*, p. 39.
[19] *Ibid.*, pp. 43-222 *passim.*
[20] Conrad Hjalmar Nordby, *The Influence of Old Norse Literature upon English Literature* (New York, 1901), p. 20.
[21] *Ibid.*, p. 24. Carlyle's later work, *The Early Kings of Norway* (1875), digests the *Heimskringla*, according to Nordby (p.26).
[22] *Ibid.*, pp. 27, 32.
[23] Stefán Einarsson, "Eirikr Magnússon and his Saga-Translations", *Scandinavian Studies and Notes*, XIII (1934), 18.
[24] Nordby, p. 32.
[25] Einarsson, p. 20n.
[26] *Collected Works*, VII, xv-xvi.
[27] C. B. Tinker and H. F. Lowry, *The Poetry of Matthew Arnold* (London, 1940), p. 90. Arnold speaks warmly of Icelandic literature in *The Study of Celtic Literature* (1867).
[28] B. Ifor Evans, *English Poetry in the Later Nineteenth Century* (London, 1933), p. xxiii.
[29] May Morris, *William Morris*, I, 440, 468.
[30] *Sigurd* (London, 1928), pp. 124-25.
[31] Mackail, I, 335.
[32] Forman, p. 48.
[33] Vaughan, p. 7.
[34] Watts-Dunton, *Athenaeum*, Dec. 9, 1876, pp. 753-54. Because of Watts-Dunton's numerous articles, I must footnote some of his utterances.
[35] *Ibid.*, p. 753.
[36] *Poetical Works of Matthew Arnold*, ed. Tinker and Lowry, p. xxiii.
[37] *Sigurd*, p. 119.
[38] Watts-Dunton, *Athenaeum*, Dec. 9, 1876, p. 754.
[39] Mackail, I, 186.
[40] May Morris, I, 475-92 *passim.*
[41] Alba H. Warren, Jr., *English Poetic Theory, 1825-65* (Princeton, 1950), p. 222.
[42] Arthur Symons, *Saturday Review*, Oct. 10, 1896, p. 388.

5. THE SOCIALIST POET

Sigurd was Morris's last sustained poetic achievement. After completing the epic in the fall of 1876, he practically quit writing poetry for seven years, and when he returned to it in 1883, his Muse had folded her wings and become a marcher in the ranks of the Socialist faithful.

Part of the reason for Morris's virtual abandonment of poetry after *Sigurd* could be said to have been that he became so occupied with public affairs that he had little time for verse-making. But Morris was never too busy to write poetry when the urge was strong enough. The probable truth of the matter is that Morris's tremendously active public life and his desertion of poetry both stemmed from the same cause: his awakened sense of responsibility to society.

In Morris's early view, the proper end of poetry was Beauty, not Truth; he considered the poet as maker, not prophet. In a letter of April, 1855 to his friend Cormell Price, contrary to George Ford's inference that he disliked Shelley for his lack of the human touch,[1] Morris rhapsodizes about Shelley's "Skylark":

> WHAT a gorgeous thing it is! utterly different to anything else I ever read: it makes one feel so different from anything else: I hope I shall be able to make you understand what I mean, for I am a sad muddle-head: I mean that most beautiful poetry, and indeed almost all beautiful writing makes one feel sad, or indignant, or—do you understand, for I can't make it any clearer; but "The Skylark" makes one feel happy only; I suppose because it is nearly all music, and that it doesn't bring up any thoughts of humanity: but I don't know either.[2]

Thus, although in a later statement (November, 1892), Morris says of the Oxford days that he liked Keats because he "represented semblances, as opposed to Shelley who had no eyes",[3] it is clear that in 1855 he greatly admired Shelley's detachment from social problems in "The Skylark"—a detachment that was unusual in Shelley's poetry. And about the same time, Morris was giving up the idea of taking Holy Orders and founding a monastery; under the stimulus of Ruskin's *Modern Painters, Seven Lamps of Architecture*, and *Stones of Venice*, Edward Burne-Jones and Morris decided to take up painting and architecture respectively.[4] The following year, Morris came under the spell of Rossetti, who persuaded him that he should paint and whose influence was probably decisive, as Margaret Grennan thinks,[5] in determining Morris to remain detached from the problems of the world and limit his attention to art.

Nevertheless, it seems evident that Morris felt a strong social concern even during his college days: witness his forementioned intention of using his fortune to found and support a monastery. Also, in addition to stimulating his desire to be an architect, the works of Ruskin, particularly *The Stones of Venice*, must have increased Morris's awareness of the unhappy condition of laborers in England. In later life, Morris credited Ruskin with leading him toward Socialism: "It was through him that I learned to give form to my discontent."[6] And Morris's Socialism always bore a distinct Ruskinian tinge. For example, one of the keynotes of Morris's doctrine, that "nothing should be made by man's labour which is not worth making, or which must be made by labour degrading to the makers",[7] is an echo of Ruskin's statement in "The Nature of Gothic" (Chapter VI, *Stones of Venice*) that the great discontent of English workmen can be eliminated "only by a right understanding, on the part of all classes, of what kinds of labour are good for men, raising them, and making them happy; by a determined sacrifice of such convenience, or beauty, or cheapness as is to be got only by the degradation of the workman; and by equally determined demand for the products and results of healthy and ennobling labour".[8]

But in his early years, Morris preferred to push social problems out of his mind. His letter of July, 1856 to Cormell Price, after mentioning his decision to take Rossetti's advice and study painting, contains the significant comment, "I can't enter into politico-social subjects with any interest, for on the whole I see that things are in a muddle, and I have no power or vocation to set them right in ever so little a degree."[9]

The similarity of this statement to the theme of the Apology to *The Earthly Paradise* is unmistakable; and although the Apology is misleading if taken as a comprehensive statement of Morris's poetic method, it is an accurate indication of his resolve not to "strive to set the crooked straight". In his first three major works, Morris's main concern is clearly not to instruct, but to present a story or picture for its own sake. *Love is Enough* marks a temporary departure from this attitude, but even so, the example of the king's action suggests the advisability of avoiding entanglement in worldly affairs; and in *Sigurd* Morris is again absorbed in the story for its own sake; the reader may find inspiration in its examples of heroic action, but by no stretch of the imagination could it be called didactic.

However, Morris was finding it difficult to remain aloof from social problems. It is fruitless to look for any sustained Socialist allegory in Morris's early poems; to say, for example, that *The Earthly Paradise* is a sermon in favor of establishing a Socialistic paradise, as Clement Shorter maintains (*Bookman*, June, 1897) along with several other retrospective critics, is sheer nonsense. But one can find occasional evidences of dissatisfaction with the existing order. In addition to the overt expressions of this dissatisfaction in the Apology:

> The heavy trouble, the bewildering care
> That weighs us down who live and earn our bread,

and in the beginning of the Prologue:

> Forget six counties overhung with smoke,
> Forget the snorting steam and piston stroke,
> Forget the spreading of the hideous town,

probably the most noteworthy piece of evidence is the passage in the Prologue where the wanderers find a shrine in a cave two-thirds of the way up the side of a mountain, in which a golden god sits on an altar surrounded by golden-crowned dead men hanging on the walls.

The same year in which Volume I of *The Earthly Paradise* appeared, Morris published "The God of the Poor" in the *Fortnightly Review* (August, 1868). A ballad-like narrative of fifty-two four-line stanzas with the refrain "*Deus est Deus pauperum*", the poem recounts how an evil lord, Maltete, is led into ambush by the lure of gold and vanquished by the good knight, Boncoeur; and it ends with the caution, "Take we heed of such-like men" (i.e., Maltete).[10] The tale is reminiscent of "Geffray Teste Noire" in *Guenevere*, but is not nearly so realistic or effective; it is noteworthy mainly as the closest approach to propagandist literature which Morris wrote before he stepped into public life.

In 1874, as his letter of March 6th to Mrs. Alfred Baldwin shows, Morris was still in the position of seeing things "in a muddle" without the power "to set them right", but one can see how strong an urge he felt to try. Speaking of the ugliness of London, he writes:

> Surely if people lived five hundred years instead of threescore and ten they would find some better way of living than in such a sordid loathsome place, but now it seems to be nobody's business to try to better things—isn't mine you see in spite of all my grumbling—but look, suppose people lived in little communities among gardens and green fields, so that you could be in the country in five minutes' walk, and had few wants, almost no furniture for instance, and no servants, and studied the (difficult) arts of enjoying life, and finding out what they really wanted: then I think one might hope civilization had really begun.[11]

The trend of Morris's thinking is clear, though he did not become an avowed Socialist for another nine years. The letter contains in germ most of the essential elements of the Socialist paradise which he would describe sixteen years later in *News from Nowhere*.

It took the crisis in the Middle East to goad Morris into public action. During 1876, Turkey's brutal suppression of the insurrection in her European provinces, and especially in Bulgaria, drew the threat of Russian intervention—a threat which became an actuality in April of 1877—and England came very close to declaring war against Russia in order to preserve the balance of power. Near the close of 1876, incensed at the prospect of an unjust war, Morris joined the recently-formed Eastern Question Association as treasurer.[12] The Manifesto which he issued on May 11, 1877, is remarkable in that it is addressed "To the Working-men of England" and contains a diatribe against capitalists which foreshadows his Socialist lectures:

> Working-men of England, one word of warning yet: I doubt if you know the bitterness of hatred against freedom and progress that lies at the hearts of a certain part of the richer classes in this country ... these men cannot speak of your order, of its

aims, of its leaders without a sneer or an insult: these men, if they had the power (may England perish rather) would thwart your just aspirations, would silence you, would deliver you bound hand and foot for ever to irresponsible capital—and these men, I say it deliberately, are the heart and soul of the party that is driving us to an unjust war....[13]

At about the same time, Morris's aesthetic sensibility, which had long been distressed by the damage that was being done to historic buildings in the name of "restoration", impelled him to found the Society for the Protection of Ancient Buildings (March, 1877) and enroll as members many influential people, including Carlyle and Ruskin; the SPAB, or "Anti-Scrape", for which Morris acted as secretary, occupied part of his attention for the rest of his life.[14] And before the end of 1877, Morris gave the first of his numerous lectures on the arts and crafts: "The Decorative Arts", delivered to the Trades Guild of Learning on December 4th, and later included in *Hopes and Fears for Art* (1882) as "The Lesser Arts".[15]

This lecture is especially interesting for three reasons: it shows Morris, more than five years before he called himself a Socialist, actually envisaging a Socialist Utopia; it shows the influence of Ruskin; and it foreshadows the peculiar (for a Socialist) orientation toward art which was to dominate Morris's Socialist arguments for the rest of his life. Morris begins the lecture by identifying the uses of the decorative arts as "to give people pleasure in the things they must perforce *use*" and "to give people pleasure in the things they must perforce *make*". For the "truest and the most eloquent words that can possibly be said" about the necessity of giving workers pleasure in their work, he refers the audience to "The Nature of Gothic" in Ruskin's *Stones of Venice* (II). The problem, as Morris sees it, is that the taste for art is dying out because of the ugliness of modern civilization: "How can I ask working-men passing up and down these hideous streets day by day to care about beauty?" What is needed for the rebirth of the arts is leisure from "war commercial, as well as war of the bullet and the bayonet ... leisure above all from the greed of money, and the craving for that overwhelming distinction that money now brings." And without identifying it as such, Morris forecasts the Socialist millennium:

> I believe that as we have even now partly achieved LIBERTY, so we shall one day achieve EQUALITY, which, and which only,

means FRATERNITY, and so have leisure from poverty and all its griping sordid cares.

Then having leisure from all these things, amidst renewed simplicity of life we shall have leisure to think about our work, that faithful daily companion, which no man any longer will venture to call the Curse of labour: for surely then we shall be happy in it, each in his place, no man grudging at another; no one bidden to be any man's *servant*, every one scorning to be any man's *master*: men will then assuredly be happy in their work, and that happiness will assuredly bring forth decorative, noble, *popular* art.[16]

This is "Socialism seen through the eyes of an artist", as Morris describes it in a letter of Sept. 5, 1883, to Andreas Scheu, the Austrian revolutionary who became prominent in the Socialist movement in Scotland. From the evidence of this lecture and the EQA Manifesto, it is clear that Morris's thinking was already Socialistic and his acceptance of Henry Hyndman's invitation to join the recently-formed Democratic Federation, then the only active organization in England with Socialist principles, was virtually inevitable. In Morris's own words to Scheu, "I always intended to join any body who distinctly called themselves socialists."[17]

Morris enrolled in the Democratic Federation (which soon added the prefix "Social" to its title) on Jan. 17, 1883, as "William Morris, designer"; in May he was elected to the executive committee, but his association with the Federation lasted less than two years. The chairman, Hyndman, had strong parliamentarian leanings whereas Morris was a revolutionist who thought the main business of Socialists was to make Socialists and stay clear of Parliament, so that an eventual split was probably inevitable;[18] but Hyndman's attempt to impose arbitrary rule forced the issue, and Morris withdrew in December of 1884 and founded the Socialist League.[19] His association with the League, which he served as treasurer—and subsidizer to the tune of as much as 500 pounds a year[20]—lasted about six years; in 1889 the Anarchists ousted him from the executive committee, and in November of 1890, Morris left the League and formed the Hammersmith Socialist Society, with which he continued till his death.[21]

In his diary entry for Sept. 30, 1891, Wilfrid Scawen Blunt says of Morris, "Politically he is in much the same position as I am. He has found his Socialism impossible and uncongenial, and has thrown it wholly up for art and poetry, his earlier loves."[22] Although the diarist was mistaken in thinking Morris had abandoned his Socialist ideals, it is true that after his withdrawal from the League, Morris practically washed his hands of militant campaigning and redirected his attention largely to art and literature. George Bernard Shaw is very close to the truth when he says, in the *Daily Chronicle* of April 20, 1899: "Morris's notions of how the changes he desired would come about altered from a point at which he saw nothing for it but a forcible overthrow ... to an attitude so Fabian that he practically left Socialism to work itself out in the ordinary course of politics."

Shaw thinks the turning-point for Morris was the "Bloody Sunday" episode of Nov. 13, 1887, when police charged into a peaceful assembly of Irish, Radicals, and Socialists in Trafalgar Square, inflicted numerous injuries, and completely routed the demonstrators. Besides being outraged at the injustice of the action, Morris was dismayed by the ease with which the rout had been accomplished. As his account of the incident in the *Commonweal* states, "I could see that numbers were of no avail unless led by a band of men acting in concert and each knowing his part."[23] Whether or not "Bloody Sunday" was the deciding factor, Morris certainly altered his earlier belief that a quick revolution was possible and came to accept the necessity of working through Parliament. In a letter of April 6, 1890, to Bruce Glasier, Scottish Socialist, Morris complains that the Anarchists "don't know anything about Socialism and go about ranting revolution in the streets, which is about as likely to happen in our time as the conversion of Englishmen from stupidity to quickwittedness."[24] And in a previously unpublished lecture of 1893, which May Morris quotes, Morris states his attitude toward parliamentarianism at this time:

> I confess I am no great lover of political tactics; the sordid squabble of an election is unpleasant enough for a straightforward man to deal in: yet I cannot fail to see that it is necessary somehow to get hold of the machine which has at its back the executive power of the country, however that may be done, and that the organization and labour which will be necessary to effect that by means of the ballot-box will, to say the least of it, be little indeed compared with what would be necessary to effect it by open revolt.... In short I do not believe in the possible success of revolt until the Socialist party

> has grown so powerful in numbers that it can gain its end by peaceful means, and that therefore what is called violence will never be needed; unless indeed the reactionaries were to refuse the decision of the ballot-box and try the matter by arms. . . .

Hitting again at the Anarchists, Morris continues:

> As to the attempt of a small minority to terrify a vast majority into accepting something which they do not understand, by spasmodic acts of violence, mostly involving the death or mutilation of noncombatants, I can call that nothing else than sheer madness. And here I will say once for all, what I have often wanted to say of late, to wit that the idea of taking any human life for any reason whatsoever is horrible and abhorrent to me.[25]

Although Morris's politics were modified in these several ways, the loss to poetry caused by his social concern was irreparable. When Morris had first decided to take an active part in public life, his Muse decisively left the Palace of Art from which she had only occasionally peeked before. He had come to the point where he considered poetry unimportant unless it served the deep needs of the day. In a letter to Georgiana Burne-Jones in October, 1879, he says, "As to poetry, I don't know, and I don't know. The verse would come easy enough if I had only a subject which would fill my heart and mind: but to write verse for the sake of writing is a crime in a man of my years and experience."[26] Writing to the same correspondent three years later, Morris puts the case more decisively. Speaking of Swinburne's *Tristram of Lyonesse*, he says that probably because of being in a bad mood, he was unable to appreciate the poem, and he continues:

> But to confess and be hanged, you know I never could sympathize with Swinburne's work; it always seemed to me to be founded on literature, not on nature. . . . Now time was when the poetry resulting from this intense study and love of literature might have been, if not the best, yet at any rate very worthy and enduring: but in these days when all the arts, even poetry, are like to be overwhelmed under the mass of material riches which civilization has made . . . but cannot use to any good purpose: in these days the issue between art, that is, the god-like part of man, and mere bestiality, is so momentous, and

the surroundings of life are so stern and unplayful, that nothing can take serious hold of people, or should do so, but that which is rooted deepest in reality and is quite at first hand....

In all this I may be quite wrong, and the lack may be in myself: I only state my opinion, I don't defend it; still less do I my own poetry.[27]

The indictment of Swinburne's poetry in this letter provides the two-edged sword which has been so often wielded against Morris because his own inspiration was usually literary. What the critics have usually failed to point out is that the statement reflects, not a blind spot, but a change in Morris's viewpoint since his social concern became uppermost, and that he included his own work in the category of literary poetry. His position is made abundantly clear in another letter to Mrs. Burne-Jones on Aug. 21, 1883, in which he explains that he does not consider his poetry to have been "of any value except to myself" and that his anxiety about his daughter Jenny's health is "too strong and disquieting to be overcome by a mere inclination to do what I *know* is unimportant work."[28] In the light of this new viewpoint, it is not surprising that after Morris resumed the writing of poetry the following month, his production was mostly limited to Socialist verse.

From 1883 to 1890, Morris's most active period of Socialism, he was extremely energetic in serving the "Cause". Besides giving frequent lectures, some of which were published under the title *Signs of Change* (1888), he composed a number of poems which were set to familiar tunes and periodically issued in pamphlet-form as *Chants for Socialists*, as well as several additional short poems and a narrative poem in thirteen books entitled *Pilgrims of Hope* (privately printed by Harry Buxton Forman in 1886); and he wrote numerous articles, first for *Justice*, the organ of the Social Democratic Federation, and later for the Socialist League's periodical, *Commonweal*, for which he also served as editor until the Anarchists seized control of the League.[29] In addition, Morris wrote two propagandist romances: in *A Dream of John Ball*, the narrator, dreaming that he is living in the time of Wat Tyler and the Peasants' Revolt, tells the rebel-priest John Ball of the era of even greater slavery which will occur in the nineteenth century and which will eventually be abolished by the Socialist revolution; and in *News from Nowhere*, the dreamer finds himself in the post-revolution paradise, consisting mostly of rural communities, where crime is virtually non-existent, machines are used only for distasteful tasks, and everyone is more or less an artisan. *John Ball* appeared in the *Commonweal* from November, 1886, to January, 1887, and was republished in 1888 by Reeves and Turner, along with a short moralistic tale called "A King's Lesson"; and *News from Nowhere*, after running from January to October, 1890, in the *Commonweal*, was issued by the same publishers in 1891.[30]

After he left the League, Morris's Socialist activity was mostly confined to giving an occasional lecture and conducting meetings of the Hammersmith Socialist Society at Kelmscott House. His only substantial literary contribution to the Cause during this time was *Socialism, its Growth and Outcome* (1893), written in collaboration with Belfort Bax. His reawakened interest in literature asserted itself in various directions: book-collecting, printing (he founded the Kelmscott Press in 1891),[31] translation (*The Saga Library*, 1891-95, *Beowulf*, 1895, and some of the old French romances, 1893-95),[32] and the writing of original prose romances. Morris never resumed the writing of poetry, however, on any substantial scale; the *House of the Wolfings* (1889) is narrated in prose, with important speeches versified in the metre of *Sigurd the Volsung*, but Morris did not repeat the experiment: in the seven following romances (including *News from Nowhere*), the only poetry is an occasional song or an especially important oration.

There was no regular edition of Morris's Socialist verse, but he included ten of his poems for the Cause in his last volume of poetry, *Poems by the Way* (1891). As the title suggests, the book is a hodge-podge of poems which Morris had written through the years, and many of them had already appeared in various publications. The only poem written especially for this volume is the 700-line romance, "Goldilocks and Goldilocks", which Morris is reported to have composed in a single day, simply to fill out the book. Except for the inconsequential little verses written for pictures, tapestries, and embroidery, some of which had been printed in various exhibition catalogues, all the poems in Morris's last book of poetry were written either before 1874 or after 1883.[33] The earlier poems fall into two groups: those produced under the Middle-English influence (lovelyrics, ballads, and romances written during the *Earthly Paradise* period) and those which resulted from the Northern influence (ballad-like narratives based on or translated from Danish and

THE SOCIALIST POET 91

Icelandic originals). The post-1883 group contains a couple of medievalist romances, like "Goldilocks and Goldilocks", and several lyrics, but consists in the main of the Socialist verse.

Poems by the Way was reissued once (1892) before its inclusion in the *Poetical Works* of 1896;[34] but it made little impression on the critics: a half-dozen literary journals devoted a total of no more than a dozen pages to the book on its first appearance, and thereafter it received only a very occasional, and usually perfunctory, mention in articles dealing with Morris's poetry. The tepid reception, entirely understandable, can be attributed to four causes. First, as the critics recognized, *Poems by the Way* contains hardly anything new and consequently represents no development in Morris's art. Second, the quality of the poems is very uneven: there are some beautiful lyrics, such as "Meeting in Winter" (from the unpublished *Earthly Paradise* tale, "Orpheus")[35] and "Thunder in the Garden", and several very fine narratives, such as "The Wooing of Hallbiorn the Strong" and "Hafbur and Signy"; but the merit of these is counter-balanced by, on the one hand, the slightness of the small verses for pictures, tapestries, and embroidery, and on the other, the markedly inferior quality of the Socialist poetry. Third, most of the good narrative poems are labelled as translations from the Danish or Icelandic—"Hallbiorn" and "The King of Denmark's Sons" are the only exceptions—and thus can hardly be considered original. And finally, it is very likely that the mere fact that Morris included Socialist verse in the volume prejudiced some critics against it.

I do not propose to give a detailed analysis of the critical reaction to *Poems by the Way*, for not only did the critics have little to say about it, but what they did say concerning the non-didactic poems (their commentary on the Socialist poems I shall discuss later) contained nothing that had not been said more fully about Morris's earlier work. The tone of the reviews was generally favorable, but they seldom dealt in particulars. Much of the comment consisted of generalities carried over from earlier Morris criticism, often not substantiated by specific references and sometimes erroneously applied. For example, several reviews, like that in the *Speaker* of Jan. 30, 1892, named the "Muse of the North" as the chief source of inspiration for *Poems by the Way*—which the earlier description of its contents shows to be plainly inaccurate—and a couple of reviewers judged that the volume should be read in a leisurely fashion, "in a lovely garden by running water" (in the words of the *Westminster Review* of July, 1892), as if they were talking about *The Earthly Paradise*, instead of a book which could be read through in an hour or so, and some of whose contents would be far from restful.

Perhaps the least supportable generalization was that made by several later critics, and unsubstantiated by any particular examples, that *Poems by the Way* was comparable in manner to *Guenevere*. The mists of nostalgia undoubtedly blurred the vision of these writers, for the only real point of similarity between the two books is that each is a collection of short poems of various kinds. Nothing in *Poems by the Way* comes near to the psychological and dramatic truth that is characteristic of such poems as "The Defence of Guenevere", "The Haystack in the Floods", and "Sir Peter Harpdon's End". The poem which comes closest to resembling anything in the earlier volume is "Goldilocks and Goldilocks", which has a plot similar to that of "Rapunzel": the male Goldilocks rescues his feminine namesake from the clutches of a witch. However, as one of the few critics to make specific observations puts in the *Saturday Review* of Feb. 6, 1892, the later poem is "a very pleasant romance in itself" but "poor Goldilocks lives but in the light of common day compared with the fairy radiance that surrounded Rapunzel and surrounds her still". Or as Saintsbury might have said it, "Goldilocks" lacks the "true Romantic vague" possessed by the earlier poem.

In addition to these comments, there was the usual praise of Morris's melodiousness, pictorial description, and narrative ability, and the usual disapproval of his diffuseness, monotony, and (still hanging on in a few commentaries) antiquarianism.

Critical notice of Morris's Socialist verse was extremely scarce throughout the period from 1883 to 1900; in fact, more than half of the critics who wrote about Morris's literary production—either verse or prose—completely ignored his politics. Of some 130 articles during this period, only about sixty spoke of his Socialism. About a third of these sixty articles were primarily concerned with Morris's non-didactic works and commented briefly on the poet's political aberration; another third were reviews of Morris's prose contributions to the Cause—*Signs of Change, John Ball, News from Nowhere,* and *Socialism, its Growth and Outcome*; and the remainder were concerned with Morris as a writer of Socialist poetry, but only half of these made specific reference to individual poems.

This neglect of Morris's Socialist poems is no doubt partly attributable to the fact that there was no regular edition of them; but even after the issuance of *Poems by the Way* made available much of the Socialist verse as Morris thought worthy of preservation, the reviewers gave it little more attention than before, and it is quite likely that some critics friendly to Morris decided that the kindest thing they could do was to ignore his Socialist poetry. Of the six reviews of *Poems by the Way*, half made no mention whatever of the songs for the Cause, and the other half quickly dismissed them as being totally without merit. Fairly representative is the statement of the *Saturday Review* (Feb. 6, 1892) that the Socialist poems, unquestionably the worst in the book, are examples of Morris's "almost pathetically crude Socialism". Without giving any space to examination of the poems under discussion, the reviewer goes on to wonder that a man of genius could really expect to substitute Arcadia for the nineteenth century, but decides that it is "no more use to argue with such dreamers" than with madmen, and he judges that it is enough to say that the Muse deserts Morris when he writes on Socialism.

In an earlier chapter I stated that a couple of critics had been so depressed by the melancholy tone of *The Earthly Paradise* that they welcomed Morris's rhyming for the Cause as an expression of hope, even though they disliked Socialism; but four-fifths of the commentary on Morris's Socialist poetry was in basic agreement with the *Saturday Review's* judgment. There was no analysis of the poems; the critics simply mentioned them and wrote them off as pitiful examples of what happened to a poet's art when he took up preaching.

An interesting fact in this connection is that several of the commentators on *Poems by the Way*, while ignoring or lightly dismissing Morris's Socialist verse, expressed a liking for "The Message of the March Wind", "Mother and Son", and "The Half of Life Gone". Apparently, they did not recognize these as Socialist-inspired; the reason is doubtless that the poems form part of the narrative *Pilgrims of Hope*, which had appeared at intervals during 1885 and 1886 in the *Commonweal* before being privately issued as a volume by Harry Buxton Forman.[36] Cast in dramatic monologue form, the three poems are largely free of the hortatory nature of most of Morris's Socialist poetry; nevertheless, each of them contains enough preaching to identify it as part of the Socialist canon. For instance, in "Mother and Son", which drew the most praise of the three for the truth with which it portrays a mother's feelings, the speaker says to her sleeping baby:

> Many a child of woman to-night is born in the town.
> The desert of folly and wrong; and of what and whence are they grown?
> Many and many an one of wont and use is born;
> For a husband is taken to bed as a hat or a ribbon is worn.
> . . . .
> O son, when wilt thou learn of those that are born of despair,
> As the fabled mud of the Nile that quickens under the sun,
> With a growth of creeping things, half dead when just begun?[37]

About the literary value of Morris's Socialist poems, one can hardly help agreeing with the majority of the critics. The Muse did desert Morris when he took to preaching. The first of Morris's *Chants for Socialists*, "The Day is Coming" (1883), is fairly representative of the rest. It is too long to quote in its entirety, but the following passage is a good sample; speaking of the England of the future, the poet says:

> There more than one in a thousand in the days that are yet to come,
> Shall have some hope of the morrow, some joy of the ancient home.
> For then, laugh not, but listen to this strange tale of mine,
> All folk that are in England shall be better lodged than swine.
> Then a man shall work and bethink him, and rejoice in the deeds of his hand,
> Nor yet come home in the even too faint and weary to stand.
> Men in that time a-coming shall work and have no fear
> For to-morrow's lack of earning and the hunger-wolf anear.
> I tell you this for a wonder, that no man then shall be glad
> Of his fellow's fall and mishap to snatch at the work he had.[38]

The poem continues in this vein for another forty lines; like all battle-songs, it abounds in exaggeration and black-and-white judgment. This kind of thing may make an effective goad for the moment, but it cannot make literature. And aside from these elements, the poem is manifestly unpoetic, because of the redundancies and prosaic passages which are used to fill the metre or match the rhyme. It can be stated with a fair amount of certainty that Morris was uncomfortable writing about abstractions; his forte was describing people, actions, and things. This is why *Pilgrims of Hope* is better than the *Chants*; Morris makes it into a story, with characters who are least partly realizable: two young lovers marry and go to London, where the husband (whose name is Richard, we learn in Book VII; the wife's name is not given) joins the Socialist movement; a young gentleman named Arthur also joins the movement and falls in love with Richard's wife, who reciprocates the feeling;[39] the three take part in the Paris Commune, in which the wife and her lover are killed; and Richard returns to England to raise his son and prepare him for the coming struggle. Besides possessing characters and a story, the poem contains, especially in the three parts reprinted in *Poems by the Way*, some fine passages of description. But the story-line fumbles along and often descends to melodrama, and the characters rise above their puppet status only at rare moments, because Morris manipulates story and characters to suit his propagandist purpose; and with it all, there is the occasional inevitable preaching.

It would be impossible, of course, to make an accurate estimate of the effect which Morris's poems for the Cause had upon the rank and file of the movement, but the *Chants* were handed out to be sung at meetings, and the effect of these at least was probably considerable. This was, after all, what Morris was aiming for, rather than literary excellence. As E. P. Thompson admits, in his well-documented but Marxist-slanted biography, Morris wrote the *Chants* and *Pilgrims of Hope* not for critics or posterity, but for the day-to-day needs of the movement.[40] It would be surprising if Morris did attach lasting value to his didactic poems, for he disliked rhetoric in poetry: he said he did not care for Milton because of the rhetorical quality of his verse.[41] And it appears that Morris did not think most of his Socialist verse had any enduring literary quality; the best of his poems for the Cause, *Pilgrims of Hope*, he refused to publish as a volume, saying that it would need much revision first.[42]

Several other men of letters connected with the movement also seem to have had small regard for the literary value of Morris's Socialist poems. Oscar Wilde, who in 1891 became interested enough in Socialism to speak at a meeting and write "The Soul of Man under Socialism" (*Fortnightly Review*, February, 1891),[43] wrote a review of *Chants of Labour: A Song-Book of the People* (1889), in which several of Morris's songs appeared. In the *Pall Mall Gazette* of Feb. 15, 1889, Wilde states that the songs have no high literary value, since they are meant to be sung instead of read, but that they are no doubt effective for their purpose. It would have been cause for amazement if Wilde had expressed any higher opinion of the songs, feeling as he did that poetry should be concerned only with beauty and that preaching should be confined to prose.

Another Aesthete, W. B. Yeats, attended quite a few meetings at Kelmscott House, and he evidently read much of Morris's revolutionist verse, for his letter to Katharine Tynan in the summer of 1887 says, "I send you Morris's Socialist poems in case you have not seen them."[44] But his opinion of their literary value must have been slight, because he made no mention of them whenever he discussed Morris's works, and he valued Morris chiefly for the vision of beauty evoked by his non-didactic writings. In "The Happiest of the Poets" (*Fortnightly Review*, March, 1903), Yeats suggests that Morris's best service to the Cause was in holding up his vision of the Earthly Paradise beside modern civilization and thus showing how faded were the colors of life in his day.[45]

Similarly, in *William Morris as I Knew Him* (1936), George Bernard Shaw, who was very active in the Socialist movement, says nothing of the didactic poetry and judges that Morris's great value to the Cause came from his "unique written lectures" which revealed "his vision of the life to come on a happy earth, and his values that went so much deeper into eternity than the surplus value of Marx".[46]

Equally unfavorable as the commentary on Morris's Socialist verse was the tenor of approximately forty articles which discussed his politics without mentioning his rhymes for the Cause. Several reviews of *John Ball* and *News from Nowhere* had praise for the artistic qualities of the two romances, for they do have real stories with some good characterization, but at the same time the reviewers usually decried Morris's politics. For instance, Theodore Watts-Dunton, in his review of *John Ball* (*Athenaeum*, Dec. 22, 1888), is extravagant in his praise of "the perfect truth and beauty of the literary form" and commends Morris for his "great and generous heart", but states that Socialists in general need "more knowledge and less zeal. It is possible to see . . . that the social organism is far from being what it ought to be, and at the same time to remember that man is a creature of slow growth." It took ages for man to lose his tail, says Watts-Dunton; the Socialists would have cut it off and let the organism bleed to death.

THE SOCIALIST POET

This is a fairly good example of the dominant attitude expressed by the critics toward Morris's Socialism. Most of them considered it unrealistic, and a good number thought it was dangerous; at the same time many of them acknowledged the generosity of Morris's motives. The worst thing about Morris's enthusiasm for the movement, in the minds of a good many critics, was that it wasted his genius. Shaw, on the contrary, thinks that Morris's genius attained its fullest expression after he became a Socialist, and that his "re-writing all the old stories in very lovely verses" was merely "the prophet instinctively training himself by literary exercises for his future work".[47] Verse came too easily to Morris and did not take him to his limit, according to Shaw, but his writings about Socialism, "which the most uppish of his friends regarded as a deplorable waste of the time and genius of a great artist, really called up all his mental reserves for the first time".[48] This may be—and probably is—quite true; but I think few modern critics would assert that the amount of labor that goes into a composition is an accurate index of its literary value. None of Morris's writings for the Cause comes near the artistic quality of his major poetic works; and even Shaw admits that, during Morris's "training" period, he produced the "greatest epic since Homer, *Sigurd the Volsung*".[49]

As should be plain from the evidence already examined, the great majority of critics who wrote about Morris's Socialist writings would not have agreed with Shaw about the worth of those writings. They felt that Morris was hurting his literary reputation and wished that he would return to his true vocation, non-didactic literature. In September of 1885, when eight Socialists were arrested for obstructing a thoroughfare, Morris cried "Shame!" in Police Court and was charged with disorderly conduct and striking a policeman—a trumped-up charge which the magistrate quickly dismissed.[50] A few days later, the *Saturday Review* (Sept. 26, 1885) contained a poem by H. D. Traill entitled "The Poet in the Police Court". Addressing the Muses, Traill says:

> And the high gods designed your graceful poet
> To sing, not croak,—for swan and not for frog;
> Nor, so designing, will they if they know it,
> Let him unpunished play the demagogue.
>
> Him they intended, past all sort of doubt,
> To rhyme of old-world legend and Greek myth,

> Not to run Quixote-tilts at Adam Smith,
> Not to orate among the rabble rout
> Of knaves and loafers that you see him with,
> The ring of this last pugilistic bout. ...
> . . . .
> Take him from things he knoweth not the hang of,
> Relume his fancy and snuff out his "views,"
> And in the real Paradise he sang of
> Bid him forget the shadow he pursues.

The incident was equally shocking to the novelist, George Gissing, who was, however, more sympathetic to Morris, partly because of his own interest in Socialism, which led him to attend meetings at Kelmscott House for a time. Writing to his brother on Sept. 22, 1885, Gissing laments, "But, alas, what the devil is such a man doing in that galley? It is painful to me beyond expression. Why cannot he write poetry in the shade? ... Keep apart, keep apart, and preserve one's soul alive—that is the teaching for the day. It is ill to have been born in these times, but one can make a world within the world."[51] And it is worth noting that Gissing's feeling was shared by Morris's closest friend, Edward Burne-Jones; in a letter to an unidentified correspondent, written after Morris joined the Democratic Federation, the painter says, "I shall never try again to leave the world that I can control to my heart's desire—the little world that has the walls of my workroom for its farthest horizon;—and I want Morris back to it, and want him to write divine books and leave the rest."[52]

Although most of the critics couched their opinions in less offensive language than Traill, his poem is an accurate expression of the majority view. More typical of the wording of these writers is the statement of the *Fortnightly Review* of May 1, 1890; speaking of possible choices for the laureateship (two years before Tennyson's death), the writer says that ten or twelve years earlier, Morris would have been "a formidable competitor for any one save Lord Tennyson himself. But Mr. William Morris has renounced his calling.... He has deprived us of a good poet, and given us in exchange a preacher of Socialist homilies, not even particularly good of their kind.... No doubt he is of opinion that his present gods are worth the sacrifice. In this opinion, however, he is assuredly not supported by the majority of his readers, who will not be consoled for Medea and Gudrun,

Sigurd and Brynhild, by John Ball or the 'Kindreds of the Mark.'" A considerable number of critics had, in the *Earthly Paradise* days, tried to coax Morris out of his Palace of Art; but now that he was unquestionably out, they wanted to shoo him back inside.

The evidence presented in this chapter fully warrants, I believe, the conclusion that the total effect of Morris's Socialism on his poetic reputation was negative, rather than positive. The revolutionist poetry alone was bad enough to injure the reputation of any but the most insignificant poet; however, had he contributed nothing more to the Cause than the Socialist poems, little damage would have been done, for they could have been successfully ignored—as they in fact were by the great majority of critics—since only a few of them appeared in a regular edition of poetry. What could not so easily be overlooked, although more than half the critics did overlook it, was Morris's energetic practical work for the movement—organizing, lecturing, bailing out comrades—and his four substantial Socialist publications in prose.

Nevertheless, the damage to Morris's poetic reputation, insofar as such a thing can be calculated, was less than might have been supposed, simply because he was a poet and artist. As I stated earlier, a large number of critics respected the generosity of Morris's motives; in explaining how Morris came to be converted, some of these took the position that, as a poet, he was especially susceptible to sympathy with humanity. In the words of the *Spectator* of Oct. 10, 1885, "A poet is above all men an enthusiast, and ... of all enthusiasms the enthusiasm of humanity is the most absorbing to poetic sensibilities." The same enthusiasm, the writer reminds his readers, inspired Coleridge, Southey, Byron, and Shelley; Swinburne too has been touched by the enthusiasm of humanity, but, unlike Morris, he prefers to confine his efforts to poetry and leave the fighting to others. In this last connection, the writer was more accurate than he probably realized: in November of 1883, Morris invited Swinburne to join the Democratic Federation, but Swinburne declined, saying, "I do trust you will not ... regard me as a dilettante democrat if I say that I would rather not join any Federation. What good I can do to the cause ... will I think be done as well or better from an independent point of action and of view."[53]

Other critics explained Morris's espousal of Socialism as deriving from his love of Beauty and his desire to make it available to all men;

confronted by the ugliness of modern civilization and becoming convinced that art was being blighted by the capitalist system, according to this explanation, Morris decided that the only remedy was destruction of that system. It is clear, I think, from my discussion of Morris's progress toward Socialism, that both views have a share of the truth.

Finally, the attitude was expressed by a few critics that, in the words of Maurice Hewlett, in his review of *News from Nowhere* (*National Review*, August, 1891), "it is as ungracious as idle to argue with a poet. We must be thankful for what is best in him and give him his full meed of rope."

Thus, the final estimate must be that Morris's poetic reputation suffered a certain amount of damage from his Socialism, but that the damage was not very great. More than half the critics from 1883 to 1900 passed over his politics entirely, and most of those who decried his politics did so as good parents would correct an errant child, hating the fault, but loving and understanding the offender. It is doubtful if Morris's Socialism detracted much from the critical appreciation of his major poetic works. As the earlier chapters have shown, *Love is Enough* had already sunk into oblivion before Morris entered public life; and at the end of the century, *Guenevere* had attained something like its proper recognition, and *Jason*, *The Earthly Paradise*, and *Sigurd* remained very high in the estimation of the critics.

NOTES TO CHAPTER FIVE

[1] George Ford, *Keats and the Victorians* (New Haven, 1944), p. 151.
[2] *Letters of William Morris to his Family and Friends*, ed. Philip Henderson (London, 1950), p. 9.
[3] *Collected Works*, XXII, xxxi.
[4] Mackail, *Life of William Morris*, I, 46, 78.
[5] Margaret Grennan, *William Morris: Medievalist and Revolutionary* (New York, 1945), p. 33.
[6] "How I Became a Socialist", *Justice*, June 16, 1894, in *Collected Works*, XXIII, 279.
[7] "Art and Socialism" (1884), in *Collected Works*, XXIII, 205.
[8] Ruskin, *Works*, ed. E. T. Cook and A. Wedderburn (London, 1903-12), X, 196.
[9] *Letters of William Morris*, p. 17.

10   *Collected Works*, IX, 163.
11   *Letters of William Morris*, pp. 61-62.
12   Mackail, I, 347.
13   *Letters of William Morris*, Appendix II, pp. 388-89.
14   May Morris, *William Morris*, I, 81-82.
15   *Collected Works*, XVI, xi.
16   *Ibid.*, XXII, 3-27 *passim.*
17   *Letters of William Morris*, pp. 187-88.
18   In *News from Nowhere* (London, 1906, p. 48), Parliament is used as a storage-place for manure.
19   Mackail, II, 87-129 *passim.*
20   See letter of March 19, 1890, to Bruce Glasier, *Letters of William Morris*, p. 321.
21   Mackail, II, 238-40.
22   Wilfred Scawen Blunt, *My Diaries* (New York, 1922), Part I, p. 57.
23   May Morris, II, 252.
24   *Letters of William Morris*, p. 322.
25   May Morris, II, 350-51.
26   *Letters of William Morris*, p. 132.
27   *Ibid.*, pp. 158-59.
28   *Ibid.*, p. 180.
29   Mackail, II, 112-40 *passim.*
30   C. E. Vaughan, *Bibliographies*, p. 9.
31   Mackail, II, 253, 311-12.
32   Vaughan, p. 9.
33   *Collected Works*, IX, xxxiv-vii.
34   Vaughan, p. 7.
35   *Collected Works*, IX, xxxv.
36   *Collected Works*, IX, xxxv-vi.
37   *Ibid.*, IX, 152.
38   *Ibid.*, IX, 180.
39   The triangle of course recalls Morris's own menage and D. G. Rossetti.
40   E. P. Thompson, *William Morris: Romantic to Revolutionary* (London, 1955), p. 774.
41   *Collected Works*, XXII, xxxi.
42   Forman, Preface to *Pilgrims of Hope* (Portland, Maine, 1901), p. vii.
43   Hesketh Pearson, *Oscar Wilde* (New York, 1946). p. 138.
44   *Letters of W. B. Yeats*, ed. Allan Wade (New York, 1955), p. 47.
45   W. B. Yeats, "The Happiest of the Poets", *Fortnightly Review*, LXXIX (March, 1903), 541.
46   Shaw, *William Morris as I Knew Him* (New York, 1936), p. 50.
47   Shaw, "Keats", *The John Keats Memorial Volume* (London, 1921), in Shaw, *Collected Works*, XXIX, 191.
48   Shaw, *William Morris*, pp. 46-47.
49   *Ibid.*, p. 48.
50   Mackail, II, 146-47.
51   *Letters of George Gissing to Members of his Family*, ed. Algernon and Ellen Gissing (Boston, 1927), pp. 170, 174.
52   Georgiana Burne-Jones, *Memorials of Edward Burne-Jones* (London, 1906), p. 98.
53   Thompson, p. 312.

6. THE PROSE POET

In the fall of 1886, while William Morris was still deeply involved with Socialism, he gratified his urge to create imaginative literature and at the same time could feel that he was doing constructive work for the Cause, when he wrote his first full-length prose romance, *A Dream of John Ball* (published in book form in 1888).[1]

John Ball is definitely superior to any of Morris's Socialist poetry, because it does have a story line and good characterization of the rebel-priest, instead of being mere propaganda. As I have stated more briefly in the previous chapter, the nineteenth-century narrator relates his experiences during a dream-visit to fourteenth-century England at the time of the Peasants' Rebellion. The action is very simple: the narrator joins a group of peasants to hear an address by John Ball, he witnesses a skirmish between peasants and noblemen, he attends supper at the house of Will Green, one of the peasant leaders, and he goes to the church with John Ball to prepare for the funeral of those killed in the skirmish. During the long conversation that follows, John Ball makes several moving speeches, but the dialogue descends to obvious propaganda toward the close when the narrator speaks of nineteenth-century wage slavery and the Revolution which will end it.

Writing *John Ball* probably whetted Morris's appetite for the production of purely imaginative literature, for early in 1888, he began work on *The House of the Wolfings*, and it was published in December of the same year.[2] For the rest of his life he was almost continually at work on one romance or another. *The Roots of the Mountains* appeared in 1889; both *News from Nowhere* (his other Socialist romance) and *The Story of the Glittering Plain* came out in periodicals in 1890 and were published as books in 1891; *The Wood Beyond the World* was published in 1894; *The Well at the World's End* in 1896; and *The Water of the Wondrous Isles* and *The Sundering Flood* both appeared posthumously in 1897.[3]

In the first of his pure romances, *The House of the Wolfings*, Morris tried something new, at least for his time: he wrote the narrative in prose and nearly all the dialogue in verse. He may have felt that the technique was unsound, for he virtually abandoned verse in the later romances. Despite the sense of unreality conveyed by the mixed technique, especially at the beginning, *The House of the Wolfings* is probably the best of Morris's romances. It is imbued with the heroic atmosphere of *Sigurd the Volsung*; indeed, the word "romance" hardly fits the work, and if it were all in verse, it would certainly be called an epic.

The story is concerned with the attempts of an early Gothic tribe to repel the invasion of the Romans, and more specifically with the heroic actions of Thiodolf, war-duke of the Wolfings. Loved by the Wood-Sun, a daughter of the gods, he accepts her gift of a charmed hauberk. When he learns that the hauberk will protect him only at the expense of his people's freedom, Thiodolf fights without it and leads the Wolfings to victory, but receives his death wound in the battle.

The Roots of the Mountains is of another order. Lacking the concentration of *House of the Wolfings*, it is filled with expository and descriptive passages, and whole chapters are given to discussion of possible alternative actions. Again, it is concerned with the early Gothic tribes, this time threatened by the Huns. But the dominant interest is in the love triangle, which becomes a quadrangle. Face-of-God, son of the Alderman of Burgdale, is betrothed to a girl called the Bride, but falls in love with the Sun-Beam, princess of a mountain tribe. His new love persuades Face-of-God to enlist the aid of the Burgdalers in fighting the Dusky Men, who have driven her people from their rightful home in Silverdale. After almost endless planning and talking, the battle is finally joined, the Dusky Men are overthrown, and Face-of-God settles down in Silverdale with the Sun-Beam, while her brother Folk-Might marries the Bride and returns to Burgdale.

Roots of the Mountains, like *House of the Wolfings*, has the air of Norse saga, but in the much more compressed *Story of the Glittering Plain* Morris returned to medieval romance; in fact the tale is reminiscent of the *Roman de la Rose*. Hallblithe, of the House of the Raven, travels to the Land of the Glittering Plain in search of his kidnapped "trothplight maid" named the Hostage, whose family, significantly, is the House of the Rose. The Land is an earthly paradise (again that theme which so often occupied Morris) where people regain their youth, and where peace prevails because every man has all that he needs—which is the only suggestion of a Socialistic moral—but Hallblithe is not content to remain; in fact, he refuses to marry the Undying King's daughter who has lured him there for that purpose by sending him a lying dream. After another dream (presumably sent by the Hostage), in which he sees himself in a boat, Hallblithe sails to the Isle of Ransom and is reunited with his love.

News from Nowhere shared with *John Ball* the widest audience enjoyed by any of Morris's prose works during the last decade of the century (each had seven printings before 1900),[4] and today, when Morris is better known as a Socialist spokesman than as a poet, it is his only work that is well known. Doubtless, the reason is the theme of the book rather than its literary merit, for it cannot rank with most of the pure romances in artistry. At the same time, like *John Ball*, it is superior to any of his Socialist poems with their strident preaching.

Again Morris makes use of the dream vision, but this time the narrator finds himself in the future. The story line is slight, dealing mainly with the narrator's gradual discovery of the nature of the (this time Socialist) paradise in which he finds himself. As in most Utopian societies, there is no government to speak of because crime is almost non-existent; money is unnecessary; and the people are healthy because they are happy. What makes Morris's Socialist state really distinctive is his emphasis on the widespread aesthetic impulse everywhere evident: there is no Fine Art as such, but the people themselves express their creativity by making useful objects that are also beautiful. The Ruskinian influence which showed itself repeatedly in Morris's lectures for the Cause was never more evident than in *News from Nowhere*.

The Wood Beyond the World returns to the land of fairy romance. Golden Walter, drawn by magic to a strange land, meets a beautiful maiden by a stream and immediately falls in love with her, as she with him. The maiden is a thrall to an evil but beautiful Lady, who has drawn Walter there to make him her lover. After causing the Lady, by trickery, to kill herself, the maiden flees with Walter. The story, with its similarity to the Rapunzel theme but with sufficient variations and additions (including sex between Walter and the Witch-Lady), is concisely and skillfully told.

The reverse is true of *The Well at the World's End*, the longest of Morris's romances (two full volumes of the *Collected Works*). The story tediously follows the ramblings of Ralph, a prince, in search of the magic Well which restores youth, though it does not grant immortality. After many adventures, including a love affair with the Lady of Abundance which ends at her death, he finds the Well in the company of a second love, Ursula, daughter of a tavern-keeper. Handled with greater economy, the story could have been a success, for the love affairs are presented with realism and poignancy, but Morris perhaps lost his sense of proportion in his last years.

He did not lose his imagination, however, as *The Water of the Wondrous Isles* proves. The basic situation contains various well-tried devices of the fairytale: the child Birdalone stolen from her mother and raised by a witch; the beautiful woman named Habundia (suggesting the Lady of Abundance of the preceding romance), whom Birdalone meets in the wood and who acts like a fairy godmother; the magic ring of invisibility which Habundia gives to Birdalone. But the story contains many original ideas as well: for example, the Sending Boat, powered by blood and incantation, in which Birdalone escapes from the witch; and the various Wondrous Isles she discovers: the Isle of Young and Old, inhabited only by children and old men; the Isle of Increase Unsought, where everything grows without tillage; the Isle of the Queens, where women like statues mourn a dead king; and the Isle of the Kings, where men endlessly mourn a dead queen.

Although *The Water of the Wondrous Isles* was published after Morris's death, he had already begun to see it through the press, so that it shows little evidence of a lack of finish.[5] The case is otherwise with *The Sundering Flood*, which was published later in 1897 from the rough draft.[6] Among various defects, the most notable is that the narrator from the "House of the Black Canons" begins the story, but fades out, never to reappear. The idea of a young boy and girl trysting on opposite sides of a stream, through the years of childhood and adolescence, arouses interest at first, but the interest wanes through Childe Osberne's somewhat commonplace adventures and his eventual winning of the maid.

Morris's two Socialist romances, as might be expected, did not receive critical acclaim, although they were being widely read, probably by the working class. *John Ball* received three reviews at its publication in book form, and *News from Nowhere* five; and in the voluminous reconsideration of Morris during the four years following his death in 1896, they were virtually ignored, like his Socialist poetry. It was thus more a matter of neglect than of abuse; the critics probably felt that it would be kinder not to draw attention to his Socialist creations and to concentrate on his real achievement in non-didactic literature.

Of the reviews that were given to the two works, however, few were decidedly unfavorable. Two of the articles on *John Ball*, though brief, show a distinct attempt to find merit in the work: the writers apologetically admit that the book has a Socialistic tinge, but admire Morris's ability to recreate the England of the fourteenth-century. Theodore Watts-Dunton, Swinburne's comrade who always admired Morris, goes much further—probably too far. In the *Athenaeum* of Dec. 22, 1888, after extolling Morris as the one poet "who on all occasions produces pure poetry, and nothing else," Watts-Dunton disputes the premises of Socialism, but says that even the Socialism of Morris is far different from the common sort. The Morrisian genius he visualizes as "Titania floating and dancing among clowns". By idealizing both the past and the future "and mixing the two idealizations into one delicious amalgam, the poet of the 'Earthly Paradise' gives us the Morrisian socialism, the most charming, and in many respects the most marvellous product of 'the poet's mind' that has ever yet been presented to an admiring world". Moreover, Morris's command of medieval English, according to Watts-Dunton, gives his story a dramatic truth that even Scott failed to achieve.

Reviewing *News from Nowhere* in the *Athenaeum* of June 13, 1891, Watts-Dunton shows less enthusiasm—perhaps because the second romance uses more modern language, in keeping with its futuristic setting. The critic is more concerned than formerly with excusing Morris's "mistake", which he considers the same error "into which Shelley fell, and Victor Hugo, and other high-minded dreamers—the mistake of over-estimating man's position in the universe". Morris's place is "amongst the most visionary, and therefore the most poetic, of poets", in Watts-Dunton's view, and the critic ends on a note of praise for Morris's originality and fine descriptive writing.

Watts-Dunton's opinion of *News from Nowhere* is fairly representative of the other reviews. The *Speaker* of May 9, 1891, for example, says that Morris is "saved from the absurdities of his position by the fact that he is a poet", and expresses admiration for the "word pictures" in Morris's description of the Thames.

The critical neglect of Morris's Socialistic romances is understandable, but his other seven romances did not fare much better. *The House of the Wolfings* received six reviews; *The Roots of the Mountains* four; *The Story of the Glittering Plain* three; *The Wood Beyond the World* three; *The Well at the World's End* three; *The Water of the Wondrous Isles* five; and *The Sundering Flood* three. In addition, the romances received mention (usually brief and general) in some fifteen articles or books devoted mainly to other aspects of Morris's work or to literature in general. However, during the same period, 1889 to 1900, there were approximately sixty articles on Morris which made no reference at all to his prose fiction; we may, therefore, conclude that three-fifths of the critics were either unaware of the romances or considered them negligible.

But the picture is even less favorable than the preceding figures indicate when one considers the authorship of the signed articles (half were anonymous). Out of a total of about eighty pages devoted to the seven romances, more than one-fourth were contained in seven fat articles by Theodore Watts-Dunton, who was conducting a one-man campaign to enshrine Morris in the pantheon of great fiction-writers. Of the three reviews of *Well at the World's End*, one was contributed by an old friend, and one by an admiring acquaintance of Morris's later years: in *Nineteenth Century* (November, 1896), Swinburne terms *Well* a masterpiece—which it clearly is not; and in the *Bookman* of the same date, W. B. Yeats, without saying anything specific, finds "little details of happiness" throughout the work. And another long-time acquaintance and admirer of Morris, Harry Buxton Forman, contributed an article (*Illustrated London News*, Oct. 10, 1896) and a book (*The Books of William Morris Described*, 1897) in which the assertion is made that Morris's prose romances would be enough in themselves to assure his immortality. Thus, half of the identifiable articles (and one-fourth of the total) were written by friends or admiring acquaintances of Morris.

Another block of four commentaries was contributed by two writers of the Aesthetic Movement, Oscar Wilde and Arthur Symons, and by the aesthetic critic, George Saintsbury—predictably, for the Aesthetes usually traced their movement back to the so-called Pre-Raphaelite poets, Rossetti, Morris and Swinburne. Wilde, in a review of *House of the Wolfings* (*Pall Mall Gazette*, March 2, 1889), calls the book "a piece of pure art workmanship from beginning to end". Symons, reviewing *The Water of the Wondrous Isles* (*Saturday Review*, Dec. 11, 1897), says that Morris was "never more truly a poet than when he wrote in prose". And Saintsbury, in two of his books (*Corrected Impressions*, 1895, and *A Short History of English Literature*, 1898), finds that the prose romances revive the "vague romantic charm" of Morris's earlier verse "with wonderful effect", in the wording of the latter book.[7]

It is, of course, not my intention to discount the value of the criticism referred to above—as a matter of fact, it is gratifying to know that Morris had acquired a personal cheering section in his last years—but it does reduce by one-third the number of commentaries on the romances written by disinterested critics.

The other two-thirds also praised the romances in the majority of cases; and of the total of some forty evaluations, about three-quarters were largely favorable. It would serve little purpose to analyze the reception of each romance separately, for the criticism was much more general than the evaluations of Morris's poetry had usually been, and there was a sameness in the reactions to each successive romance that had not been prevalent in the earlier criticism.

Even Watts-Dunton's series of articles shows little variety. In his review of *The House of the Wolfings* (*Athenaeum*, Sept. 14, 1889), he says nothing of such specifics as structure or characterization, but spends most of four pages in extolling the book as a completely new form of art—a prose poem. Interestingly, it is not the mixture of verse and prose that seems so remarkable to him; it is the "poetic prose", with "all the qualities of poetry, save metre.... So poetic, indeed, is the prose in this fascinating volume that even the verse, fine as it is, seems to fade in the midst of it." In fact, Watts-Dunton suggests that the book would have been even more poetic without the poetry, since the verse interruptions of the prose narrative diminish the dramatic illusion. Again, *The Roots of the Mountains* he praises (*Athenaeum*, Sept. 27, 1890) as a "prose poem," and he finds it a " great gain" that the dialogue is no longer versified, but thinks there are still a few too many lyrics, beautiful though they are, to maintain dramatic illusion. And the week after Morris's death (*Athenaeum*, Oct. 10, 1896), Watts-Dunton speaks of the romances as "poems without metre" and finds in them "enough poetic wealth adequately to endow a dozen poets".

Several other reviewers, very possibly influenced by Watts-Dunton, also spoke of the romances as prose poems. The *Speaker* (Dec. 6, 1890), in an anonymous general article on Morris, says that posterity "may have cause to ignore him as a poet in remembering him as a prose-poet". The *Spectator* review of *The Wood Beyond the World* (July 13, 1895) finds the story told in a "delightfully poetical fashion". Arthur Symons' comment on *The Water of the Wondrous Isles* that Morris was "never more truly a poet" has already been cited; and the review of Mackail's biography of Morris in *Literature* (May 6, 1899) asserts that the series of romances "forms a unique monument of poetical prose".

A quality which had been admired in most of Morris's poetry was again discovered in his romances by half a dozen critics: Morris's descriptive power. But few examples were given, and the praise was usually qualified in the same manner that had been applied to Morris's picture-making ability by some later critics of his poetry: the pictures were compared to those on tapestry—undoubtedly because Morris was well known for his manufacture of that product. Even Oscar Wilde, in his review of *House of the Wolfings* (*Pall Mall Gazette*, March 2, 1889), falls into this cliché. After praising the book's "decorative and descriptive beauties", Wilde compares the story to "some splendid old tapestry crowded with stately images and enriched with delicate and delightful detail". With Wilde, however, it is evident from his wording that the comparison is not meant to be derogatory. Nevertheless, the tapestry image is ill-suited to the epic tone of the *Wolfings*.

More representative is the observation of *Literature* (Nov. 6, 1897) that *The Water of the Wondrous Isles* is like a tapestry in the mingling of main story with episode and description. "For just as in tapestry there is little heightening of a central effect by varying strength of light or by gradual leading of the eye to a central figure, so here there is no dramatic culmination of the story, no attempt to adjust the proportionate value of incidents." Applied to the meandering and unclimactic, though interesting, *Wondrous Isles*, the comparison is not inappropriate.

The chief objection to the prose romances was one which Morris had been hearing for years in connection with his poetry: the complaint against his use of archaic diction. In his prose fiction, Morris made wider use of archaisms than in his poetry—perhaps to compensate for giving up the heightening effect of verse. The archaisms are not so frequent or unintelligible as to prevent a reader from understanding the story, but many of the critics resented Morris's use of them. Of some twenty-five commentaries which mentioned it, two-fifths found it a serious fault, and a few of them viewed it as an insurmountable obstacle to the reading of the works. The *Library* review of the *Glittering Plain* (June, 1891), for example, says the story would doubtless be interesting if it were not for the language, "which is a more effectual barrier to most readers than the majority of foreign languages". Occasionally the objection took the form of a parody, as in the *Saturday Review's* evaluation of *House of the Wolfings* (Jan. 26, 1889). Imagining himself wielding a "fool-queller" (sword) against archaisms, the reviewer says, "For of a truth it is well that each should speak in his own tongue, and not in that which is not his own, if haply it ever were the tongue of any man." Most often the complaint was peevish, as in the *Spectator* review of *Roots of the Mountains* (Feb. 8, 1890) which laments, "This is a good thing spoilt.... Mr. Morris disdains to use a good English phrase, no matter how old, that is still current."

If the objections were vehement to the point of shrillness, at least they were outnumbered by the defences of Morris's diction. In Oscar Wilde's review of *House of the Wolfings* (already cited), he finds the language deserving of praise, not blame, because its remoteness from the common language of the day "gives to the whole story a strange beauty and an unfamiliar charm.... and no shrill insistence upon a supposed necessity for absolute modernity of form can prevail against the value of a work that has the incomparable excellence of style". Another reviewer of the *Wolfings*, Henry Hewlett (*Nineteenth Century*, August, 1889), sees one of the principal charms of the work to be its re-creation of the Gothic atmosphere and finds that one of the strongest factors in this effect is Morris's prose, "a pure draught from 'the well of English undefiled'".

Similarly, aesthetic critics George Saintsbury and Arthur Symons found the diction of Morris's romances to be absolutely essential; in Symon's words (*Saturday Review*, Dec. 11, 1897), which can also be taken to represent Saintsbury's view, Morris "writes a purer English than most people.... It is sufficient justification of his style to say that it is perfectly suited to his own requirements". These examples are fairly representative of the other defences of Morris's diction.

In light of Morris's known Socialist activities and especially of his publication of *John Ball* and *News from Nowhere*, it is not surprising that some reviewers thought the other prose romances were meant to be Socialist allegory. This could be one reason for some critics' neglect of the romances; they may have thought the supposed allegories were not worth looking at, or they may have thought it kinder not to call attention to them.

The surprising thing is that so few of the critics who did write about the pure romances viewed them as allegory. Charles Elton (*Academy*, Feb. 9, 1889) sees allegory in *The House of the Wolfings*, but finds it a powerful work nevertheless. The *Spectator* reviewer of *Roots of the Mountains* (Feb. 8, 1890) finds in it a "poetical sketch of the Morrisian Millenium", though he concedes he may be mistaken. A critic writing in the *Westminster Review* (July, 1892) calls *The Story of the Glittering Plain* a Utopian romance with "genuine poetic quality and fragrance", but "hardly more imaginative than *News from Nowhere*". But after the *Spectator* review (July 13, 1895) of *Wood Beyond the World*, in which the supposed allegory is confidently worked out in detail, Morris decided to scotch all such interpretations of his non-didactic works. His letter to the *Spectator* of July 20, 1895, disavows any allegorical intention in the romance under discussion and asserts, "If I have to write or speak on social problems, I always try to be as direct as I possibly can be. On the other hand, I should consider it bad art in anyone writing an allegory not to make it clear from the first that this was his intention." Morris's statement seems to have stilled any further conjecture about hidden Socialist meaning in the romances.

In estimating what effect the prose romances had on Morris's literary reputation, we can say that they definitely added something to his stature—Yeats, for instance, says that Morris's prose fictions were "the only books I was ever to read slowly that I might not come too quickly to the end"[8]—but they did not add a great deal. The Socialist romances were widely read but, like Morris's Socialist verse, they detracted from his reputation with men of letters rather than adding to it. The non-didactic romances were never popular with the reading public, and as we have seen, although the reviews they did receive were generally favorable, still three-fifths of the critical commentaries on Morris's work between 1889 and 1900 completely overlooked his accomplishment in prose fiction.

Reasons for this neglect are difficult to assign, since several of the romances are excellent of their kind—most notably *House of the Wolfings* and *Story of the Glittering Plain*—but we can make several reasonable guesses. The liberal use of archaic diction, which a number of reviewers loudly protested, may have put off some readers and critics. Morris's known Socialism and his publication of *John Ball* and *News from Nowhere* very possibly created in some circles the misapprehension that all of the romances were propaganda, as I suggested earlier. But the most plausible and probably the most important reason is the one given by Robert Steele in the November, 1896, issue of *Tomorrow*: according to Steele, Morris's own poetry prevented his prose romances from getting adequate consideration. "It seems to have been felt that they could add little to his fame, that his genius had reached its culminating point, and that further work, however good in itself, could be considered solely in connection with the past."

NOTES TO CHAPTER SIX

[1] C. E. Vaughan, *Bibliographies*, p. 8.
[2] Morris, *Collected Works*, XIV, xxv, xxxi.
[3] Vaughan, p. 9.
[4] *Ibid.*, pp. 8-9.
[5] *Collected Works*, XX, xix.
[6] *Ibid.*, XXI, xi.
[7] George Saintsbury, *A Short History of English Literature* (London, 1898), p. 784.
[8] W. B. Yeats, *Autobiography* (New York, 1938), p. 123.

7. MORRIS AND THE REVIEWERS

From the body of commentary about Morris's poetic works, several conclusions may be drawn concerning the general critical attitude toward poetry during the period from 1858 to 1900. One noteworthy fact that emerges is that the increase of aestheticism in the production of literature in the latter third of the century was accompanied by an increase in aesthetic criticism. This was most noticeable in the Nineties, to judge from the recognition accorded *Guenevere* in that decade; but there was already an appreciable, though not yet numerous, group of aesthetic critics in the late Sixties, as evidenced by the early reviews which praised *Jason* and *The Earthly Paradise* for their simple concern with Beauty and by those which found the books a relief from the disquisitional poetry of the day.

On the other hand, it seems evident that the aesthetic critics never attained a majority position in the nineteenth century. Louise Rosenblatt states that aestheticism flourished side by side with the moralistic concept of art after 1885,[1] and it is probably true that the writers of imaginative literature were about equally divided on this question. But the same division did not hold true in criticism, as far as one can judge from the Morris commentary; the old guard continued dominant throughout the period under discussion, although the throne was being shaken late in the century by the increasing ranks of aesthetes.

In support of this contention, many critics of *Jason* and *The Earthly Paradise* complained about the poet's failure to deal in the currents of his own time and about the absence in the works of any moral instruction; and some of Morris's defenders tacitly accepted the moralistic view in asserting that instruction could be found in the poems if one looked for it. At the same time, many of those who welcomed the books as an escape from the problems of the time acknowledged that the noblest poetry was that which gave the reader renewed strength to face life's battles. And the object of one of the most widespread and least controverted complaints against Morris's most famous work was the melancholy tone, for this seemed to strike at the heart of Christianity. As Walter Houghton points out, it was assumed by most people in the Victorian period, whether or not they had any real belief themselves, that a collapse of religious faith would destroy the sanctions of morality, and with the buttress of morality gone, society would crumble.[2]

The warm approval of *Love is Enough* on its appearance is evidence of moralistic tendencies in the criticism of the early Seventies but, since the poem was quickly forgotten, tells us little about the last quarter of the century. However, the overwhelmingly favorable commentary on *Sigurd* throughout the period from 1876 to 1900, especially in its recognition that Morris was no longer an "idle singer", gives additional and strong support to my contention.

But if the majority of critics felt that the noblest poetry should either teach or inspire (while delighting, of course), they seem to have had a decided preference for the indirect method of instruction or uplift. The critical aversion to Morris's Socialist poems is hardly admissible as evidence, because the lesson was all wrong: the critics saw these poems to be aimed at the destruction, rather than the preservation, of society. The quick oblivion, however, which surrounded *Love is Enough*, whose message met with full approval, is a valid indication of this preference; and a stronger indication is the fact that a goodly number of critics considered *Sigurd*, with its inspiration by example, to be Morris's greatest poem.

In addition to these general attitudes regarding the proper end of poetry, the Morris commentary yields information about the kind of poem which was most likely to meet with critical approval during the last four decades of the century. Although some of the aesthetic critics preferred obscure and exotic lyrics, it can hardly be disputed that the great majority of reviewers preferred clear, straight-forward narrative poetry; this is shown not only by the great critical popularity of *Jason* and *The Earthly Paradise*, but also by the less numerous but more whole-hearted plaudits awarded to *Sigurd*, which even some of the aesthetic critics, like Symons, considered Morris's greatest achievement. Here was a manifest shift in attitude since the early part of the century, when the lyric, in the words of M. H.

Abrams, was thought by most theorists to be "the essentially poetic form, and usually, the type whose attributes are predicated of poetry in general".[3]

The evidence further suggests that, although a very considerable minority of later nineteenth-century reviewers liked romance, with its unhurried narrative, detailed description, flat characters and lack of dramatic intensity, a majority of the critics considered the epic to be the noblest form of poetry. In addition to the implicit evidence of this view in the criticism of *The Earthly Paradise* for its "unheroic melancholy", its weak characterization, and its lack of dramatic power, the explicit evidence of three-fourths of the *Sigurd* commentators (more than thirty out of some forty articles) would seem to be decisive. This conclusion is in accord with the findings of Donald M. Foerster (*The Fortunes of Epic Poetry*, 1962), who says that the Victorian period restored to the classical epic a great deal of the prestige it had lost during the Romantic period.[4]

Toward professional critics as a class, Morris had a contemptuous attitude. Mackail quotes him as saying, "To think of a beggar making a living by selling his opinion about other people! and fancy any one paying him for it!"[5] And in a letter to the *Pall Mall Gazette* of Nov. 1, 1886, Morris protests the proposed establishment of a Chair of English Literature, which he thinks will turn out to be really a Chair of Criticism. "For the result would be merely vague talk about literature, which would teach nothing. Each succeeding professor would strive to outdo his predecessor in 'originality' on subjects whereon nothing original remains to be said."

In keeping with this attitude, as might be expected, it has been said by a number of persons variously qualified to judge, that Morris was indifferent to criticism of his poetry. For example, Morris's friend and publisher, F. S. Ellis, says that Morris wrote spontaneously, without giving any consideration to "whether what he thought of writing would be likely to find acceptance with the public.... He wrote for art's sake, and for art's sake only."[6] And Theodore Watts-Dunton writes in the *Athenaeum* (Dec. 4, 1897) that "no other poet of our time, and perhaps no poet of any other time, ever took up as he did the purely Olympian attitude towards the literary arena". This view is supported by Wilfred Scawen Blunt's reminiscence about the manner in which Morris used to read his poems to the Oxford Brotherhood: it was not as if Morris were inviting criticism, but "as if he were throwing a bone to a dog, at the end of each piece breaking off with 'There, that's it,' as much as to say, 'You may take it or leave it, as you please'".[7]

Probably no poet in history, however, was ever completely invulnerable to brickbats. Morris was certainly less thin-skinned than many writers have been; he never felt it necessary, for instance, to make any public defence of his literary principles. His closest approach to such a defence was his letter to the *Spectator* of July 20, 1895, in which he denies the statement by the *Spectator* reviewer that *The Wood Beyond the World* is an allegory; the only reason he protests, he explains, is to call attention to an error of fact, not opinion, for "I make it a rule not to answer any criticism of my literary work, feeling that the writers have formed their opinions on ground sufficient to themselves, and that they have a full right to express those opinions." Nevertheless, there is evidence that the strictures of the critics did have an effect on Morris, especially during his earlier years; the exact extent of that effect is open to conjecture, but in the following discussion I shall try to set some general limits to such conjecture.

Even Ellis admits that Morris, in his early days, was "curious as to how his verse would be received";[8] and it is highly probable that the ungracious reception of *Guenevere* made Morris hesitate to thrust his head through the bull's-eye again (like Tennyson twenty-six years earlier), for he published nothing more until nine years later, even though he wrote a great amount of poetry during this time. This supposition is further supported by the fact that Morris evidently decided to issue *Jason* separately in order to gauge the public taste for this kind of poetry. *Jason's* immediate popularity with both public and critics gratified Morris immensely. His letter of June 20, 1867, apparently to Bell and Daldy, his publishers (Ellis became his publisher after the second edition of *Jason*),[9] exults:

> Naturally I am in good spirits after the puffs. . . . I fancy I shall do pretty well now; last week I had made up my mind that I shouldn't be able to publish "The Earthly Paradise" and was very low: I am as anxious as you are to get on with that work, and am going to set to work hard now.[10]

Thus it is very possible that, as May Morris says, if *Jason* had not been well-received, *The Earthly Paradise* "would not have seen the light in its present form, or at any rate would not have been so speedily published".[11]

It is not so easy to show, however, that the detractors of *Guenevere* "obviously dissuaded" Morris, in the words of Karl Litzenberg, from the continuance of his "Pre-Raphaelite minstrelsy".[12] As Rossetti's influence waned and Morris's strongly self-sufficient character began to assert itself, he apparently lost interest in the creation of airy little mood-pieces such as "The Blue Closet", while his interest increased in the kind of verse which, to me at least, constitutes the true value of the *Guenevere* volume: narrative and dramatic poetry. Morris was evidently torn between these two types: in *Guenevere* he had used both forms, sometimes combining them in one poem, as in "King Arthur's Tomb"; in the interval between his first and second books, he experimented with each in unmixed form: the Troy poem was to be completely dramatic, and *The Earthly Paradise* was taking shape in his mind as a series of narratives in a frame. It was not a case of trying first the dramatic, and then the narrative form, as Mackail implies,[13] for May Morris describes an 1862 notebook which contains a list of some of the scenes from the Troy poem; thus, Morris was still working on this project a year after he had written "The Watching of the Falcon" and "The Proud King", the first drafts of which appear in an 1861 notebook.[14] What finally confirmed Morris as a narrative poet was probably the success of *Jason*; had the book met with much abuse, I find it entirely conceivable that Morris's next project would have been to complete and publish the Troy poem—especially since "The Death of Paris", though its subject is not on the original list of scenes for the Trojan cycle, contains much excellent dialogue and is one of the most effective poems in *The Earthly Paradise*.

May Morris thinks there were two other contributing factors in making Morris a narrative poet: his dislike for the Victorian stage and his recognition of the incompatibility of drama and narration.[15] The first of these gains support from Morris's own statement in 1892 that his lack of sympathy with drama prevented him from appreciating Shakespeare.[16] But a poem can be written in dramatic form without being intended for the stage, and Morris's continued interest in dramatic poetry is evidenced by his composition of *Love is Enough* in this form, as May Morris concedes.[17] Her second contention is disproved by Morris's greatest work: at moments of high passion in

Sigurd, Morris achieves tragic intensity by the masterful welding of dramatic to narrative form. It is evident, then, that the three phases in Morris's technique, which Douglas Bush identifies as "the dramatic, the simply narrative and pictorial, and the epic", are not as distinct as Bush suggests.[18]

Nevertheless, *Sigurd* is basically a narrative poem, and in *Love is Enough*, one senses that Morris was more interested in the experiment of reviving the medieval morality and the alliterative measure than in writing a powerful poem. He does not appear to have set much value on it himself: May Morris reports, "Talking of early English poetry with a friend one day, he said; 'You know, I wrote an alliterative poem myself once on a time'—almost as though it had been written by someone else."[19] All of his best poetry after *Guenevere* was written in the narrative form (with the exception of occasional interspersed lyrics); it is worth noting that now it was long, straightforward narrative for the most part—the influence of the concise Browningesque monologue form, with its subtle revelation of character, had virtually disappeared. Morris once told J. Comyns Carr (the writer of several Arthurian dramas) that he did not care much for a story unless it was long;[20] and Mackail is probably correct in thinking it much more likely that Morris's medievalism and inclination toward romantic narration led him to select Chaucer as a model, than that Chaucer's influence made him into a latter-day gestour.[21]

It can be said with confidence, then, that *Jason's* success probably convinced Morris that his true calling was that of a poetic narrator of old stories. But, although one cannot say with certainty that the critics of *Guenevere* did not cause Morris to stop writing things like "The Blue Closet" or "The Haystack in the Floods", it seems more likely that the diminishing of Rossetti's and Browning's influence was really the deciding factor.

Similarly, one could deduce that the demand for a message by critics of *The Earthly Paradise* led Morris to the didacticism of *Love is Enough*, but if so, why did not the critical approval of *Love's* message persuade Morris to continue in this vein? Moreover, although *Love is Enough* points a moral, that moral is not so bland as the title implies or as the reviewers inferred. The first passage of "Music" reads:

> Love is enough: though the world be a-waning
> And the woods have no voice but the voice of complaining,[22]

and the last passage of "Music" quotes *Love* as saying

> "Come cling round about me, ye faithful who sicken
> Of the weary unrest and the world's passing fashion!"[23]

Furthermore, Pharamond retreats from the troublesome world to find bliss with his dream-lover. *Love is Enough* can be seen as one more evidence of Morris's feeling that things were in a "muddle" and he had no power to right them; the book is as much a rejection of his times as *The Earthly Paradise* with its opening exhortation to forget the ugly modern world. In saying that "love is enough", Morris almost approaches the despairing cry of Arnold's "Dover Beach":

> Ah, love, let us be true
> To one another! (29f)

since this is the only positive value in a world like

> a darkling plain
> Swept with confused alarms of struggle and flight,
> Where ignorant armies clash by night (35ff).

So that the tone of *Love is Enough* is not really very different from that of *The Earthly Paradise*, although the reviewers thought it was.

Likewise, the loud criticism of the fatalism expressed in *The Earthly Paradise* did not diminish the fatalism woven throughout *Sigurd*; true, it was now a more hopeful kind of fatalism, but the element of hope is inherent in the subject-matter and can hardly be regarded as a concession to the critics. And the fact that *Sigurd* received perhaps less acclaim than Morris thought it merited was certainly not the cause of his abandoning poetry for a time. I trust the preceding chapter has shown that Morris's social concern was responsible for his desertion of the Muse—and for her desertion of him when he wrote verses for the Cause.

When Morris returned to literature, it was to write romances in prose, not verse. Watts-Dunton attributes this to Morris's feeling, because of the reception of *Sigurd*, that poetry no longer was appreciated—a curious statement, in view of Watts-Dunton's comment about Morris's "Olympian" detachment. But *Sigurd* was very well received by the reviewers, though it did not sell as fast as Morris probably thought it should. It is true, however, that Morris was somewhat scornful of the lack of public taste for poetry; he told

Yeats in the summer of 1887 that he was only making a hundred pounds per annum from his books and denounced the public for reading nothing but scandal or the newspaper.[24] And in a letter of Aug. 27, 1894, to Philip Webb, he says of the Kelmscott Press books, "I do the books mainly for you and one or two others; the public does not really care about them a damn."[25] Nevertheless, Morris did not stop issuing books from the Kelmscott Press, and he did not stop writing poetry because of a supposed lack of public taste for it. In *The House of the Wolfings* he wrote most of the dialogue in metre, and Ellis says that Morris first composed a considerable portion of *The Water of the Wondrous Isles* in verse, but discarded it and rewrote the romance in prose.[26] Thus, it appears that Morris was not averse to metrical composition in his last years but that he now felt more comfortable in prose than in verse. The many thousands of words which he had written for the SPAB, for his art lectures, and for the Socialist Cause undoubtedly made prose-writing seem natural to him; and May Morris quotes him as saying in later life, "A man shouldn't write poetry after he is fifty."[27]

One of the most persistent faults that critics found with Morris's first three works was their antiquarianism, but the poet paid not the least attention to this complaint. Feeling as he did that an artist with a keen sense of beauty could not portray modern life as it was, he not only continued his preoccupation with the past in *Love is Enough* and *Sigurd*, but to his prose romances he imparted even more of an antique flavor than any of the poems possess, by a much wider use of archaic diction. Morris' view of language was in keeping with his view of subject-matter; his letter of Nov. 6, 1885, to Fred Henderson, an aspiring poet, puts it clearly:

> You see things have very much changed since the early days of language: once everybody who could express himself at all did so beautifully, was a poet for that occasion, because all language was beautiful. But now language is utterly degraded in our daily lives, and poets have to make a new tongue each for himself: before he can even begin his story he must elevate his means of expression from the daily jabber to which centuries of degradation have reduced it.[28]

As the preceding chapter has shown, a goodly number of reviewers of the prose romances were shrill in denunciation of the archaic diction;

but Morris knew what he wanted to do and turned a deaf ear to all such complaints.

In small matters of style, the critics very likely exerted a certain amount of influence on Morris through the years. In 1875, when Ellis persuaded Morris to re-issue *Guenevere*, the poet began to make some revisions in the text, but changed his mind and let the book come out exactly as it had first appeared, even to the printer's errors.[29] The few revisions that he made were largely metrical improvements which could have been simply the result of the mature poet's awareness of the immaturity of his early verse, rather than a reaction to criticism. Maturing poetic power was also probably responsible for the noticeable prosodic improvement evidenced by *Jason* as compared to *Guenevere*. But *The Earthly Paradise* shows a markedly smaller proportion of poor rhymes than *Jason* and, issuing as it did on the heels of its predecessor, can be considered to give evidence that the criticism of *Jason* heightened Morris's awareness of such faults. The polished versification of *Love is Enough* and *Sigurd* shows that Morris was more painstaking in this respect than he had been before; this might have been either a continuing result of earlier criticism or a signification of greater maturity, and probably it was both.

The only two books which Morris revised for later editions were *Jason* and *The Earthly Paradise*. The 1882 issue of *Jason* contains slight changes on almost every page; about half of these are corrections of imperfect rhymes, but an equal number are revisions for improved expression, as in Book VII, when Jason urges Medea to stay with him because

> "The light
> Is grey and tender yet, and in your land
> Surely the twilight, lingering long, doth stand
> 'Twixt dawn and day" (410ff).

This becomes

> "The Day is yet but blind
> Amid blind sleepers: long it is meseems
> That twilight lingers over fading dreams
> 'Twixt dawn and day,"

in order to emphasize Jason's point that no one will be awake to catch Medea in his chamber.

Morris's revisions of *The Earthly Paradise* for the 1890 edition are much fewer than those of *Jason*, no doubt because fewer changes were necessary, and the revisions are more often concerned with meaning than with imperfect rhymes. In both books, a considerable number of bad rhymes remain after revision, and some of them are of the kind which had set the reviewers' teeth on edge—for example, "palpable" and "well", "knees" and "images", "Phoenician" and "wan", "darter" and "there", "head" and "furnished". So that apparently Morris retained to the end the conviction expressed in his letter of April, 1855 to Cormell Price that if "I must lose the thought, or sacrifice the rhyme to it, I had rather do the latter and take my chance about the music of it."[30]

From the evidence, then, we can set the following limits to speculation about the influence of criticism on Morris's poetry. The brickbats hurled at *Guenevere* considerably delayed Morris's reappearance before the public and caused him to issue *Jason* as a trial balloon, whose immediate success encouraged him to push ahead with his massive work and probably confirmed him as a narrative poet. In addition, it is reasonably sure that the reviewers caused Morris to take more pains with his prosody. Beyond this, it cannot be said with certainty that the critics had any appreciable influence on Morris's poetic practice. It is possible that *Guenevere's* accusers deterred him from writing more "luminously indistinct" fantasies or short and somewhat obscure narrative and dramatic poems, but I think it more likely that the cause was the assertion of his own bent. There is also a possibility that *Love is Enough* was a concession to the demand for a message, but if it was, the message was not the kind for which the critics had been asking. Moreover, Morris's refusal to cater to critical whims in other respects leads me to doubt that *Love* was anything but the result of an experiment that Morris wanted to try and a feeling that he wanted to express. For Kingsley Amis is right in saying that it was the act of writing which Morris's nature demanded and that, when he finished one literary project, he was miserable until he started another.[31] When Morris had finished *The Earthly Paradise*, he said, "I feel rather lost at having done my book. I find now I liked working at it better than I thought. I must try to get something serious to do as soon as may be."[32] And Morris was that way throughout his life, except during his period of Socialist activity. He had to be almost continually occupied with some literary project or other; if not original work, it was translation. *Love is Enough* was the first "serious" thing he found to do after *The Earthly Paradise*.

Finally, all of the discernible critical influence on Morris had to do with manner, not matter. Although he adopted a didactic view of art during his active Socialist period, all of his important poetic works, as well as all of his non-Socialistic prose romances, are concerned with pure Beauty; and with regard to public dictation of subject-matter, Morris maintained to the end the autonomy of art.

NOTES TO CHAPTER SEVEN

[1] Louise Rosenblatt, *L'Idée de l'art pour l'art* (Paris, 1931), p. 243.
[2] Walter Houghton, *The Victorian Frame of Mind, 1830-1870* (New Haven, 1957), p. 58.
[3] M. H. Abrams, *The Mirror and the Lamp* (New York, 1953), p. 98.
[4] Donald M. Foerster, *The Fortunes of Epic Poetry* (Catholic University of America Press, 1962), p. 118.
[5] Mackail, *Life of William Morris*, I, 134.
[6] F. S. Ellis, "The Life-Work of William Morris", *Journal of the Society of Arts*, May 27, 1898, p. 624.
[7] Wilfred Scawen Blunt, *My Diaries* (New York, 1922), I, 70.
[8] Ellis, p. 624.
[9] Mackail, I, 194.
[10] *Ibid.*, I, 185.
[11] *Collected Works*, II, xiv.
[12] Karl Litzenberg, "William Morris and the Reviews", *RES*, XII (1936), 428.
[13] Mackail, I, 166.
[14] May Morris, *William Morris*, I, 392.
[15] *Ibid.*, I, 390-91.
[16] *Collected Works*, XXII, xxxi.
[17] May Morris, I, 392. Cf. Hardy's experiment with "epic drama" in *The Dynasts*. In his Preface, Hardy contends that, although dramatic compositions were originally written only for the stage, "in the course of time such a shape would reveal itself to be an eminently readable one; moreover, by dispensing with the theatre altogether, a freedom of treatment was attainable in this form that was denied where the material possibilities of stagery had to be rigorously remembered" (*The Writings of Thomas Hardy*, London, 1920, XIX, xi).
[18] Douglas Bush, *Mythology and the Romantic Tradition in English Poetry* (New York, 1957), p. 298.
[19] *Collected Works*, IX, xxxi.
[20] J. Comyns Carr, *Some Eminent Victorians* (London, 1908), p. 209.
[21] Mackail, I, 178.
[22] *Love is Enough* (Boston, 1873), p. 11.
[23] *Ibid.*, p. 119.
[24] Letter from Yeats to Katharine Tynan, *Letters of W. B. Yeats* (New York, 1955), p. 46.

[25] *Letters of William Morris*, ed. Philip Henderson (London, 1950), p. 361.
[26] Letter to Theodore Watts-Dunton, Dec. 7, 1897, in Thomas Hake and Arthur Compton-Rickett, *Life and Letters of Theodore Watts-Dunton* (London, 1916), I, 101.
[27] May Morris, I, 496.
[28] E. P. Thompson, *William Morris: Romantic to Revolutionary* (London, 1955), p. 879.
[29] *Collected Works*, I, xxii-xxv.
[30] *Letters of William Morris*, p. 8.
[31] Kingsley Amis, "Communication and the Victorian Poet", *Essays in Criticism*, IV (October, 1954), 396.
[32] Mackail, I, 210.

BIBLIOGRAPHY

I. WORKS

The standard edition of Morris is the *Collected Works* in twenty-four volumes, edited by May Morris with much biographical material in the introductions (London, 1910-15).

II. BIBLIOGRAPHY

Forman, Harry Buxton, *The Books of William Morris Described* (London, 1897).
Vaughan, C. E., *Bibliographies of Swinburne, Morris and Rossetti* (*English Association Pamphlet* No. 29, December, 1914).

III. BIOGRAPHY AND LETTERS

Bloomfield, Paul, *William Morris* (London, 1934).
Eshleman, Lloyd Wendell, *A Victorian Rebel* (New York, 1940). Reprinted in London, 1949, as *William Morris: Prophet of England's New Order* under the name of Lloyd Eric Grey, in order to exploit the rise to power of the Labour Party.
Grennan, Margaret, *William Morris: Medievalist and Revolutionary* (New York, 1945).
Mackail, J. W., *The Life of William Morris*, 2 vols. (London, 1899). Still the standard biography.
Morris, May, *William Morris, Artist, Writer, Socialist*, 2 vols. (Oxford, 1936). An excellent supplement to Mackail and to the *Collected Works*.
Morris, William, *The Letters of William Morris to his Family and Friends*, ed. Philip Henderson (London, 1950).
Thompson, E. P., *William Morris: Romantic to Revolutionary* (London, 1955).

IV. NINETEENTH-CENTURY CRITICISM

My main bibliographical source for this area has been Theodore G. Ehrsam *et al.*, *Bibliographies of Twelve Victorian Authors* (New York, 1936), which directed me to about 225 articles referring to Morris between 1858 and 1900. Browsing turned up the following additional references:

Academy, Nov. 24, 1883, p. 350.
Blackwood's, CVII (May, 1870), 644-47.
Morley, Henry, *Of English Literature in the Reign of Victoria* (London, 1881), p. 410.
Saturday Review, Dec. 24, 1870, pp. 808-9.
———, July 17, 1875, pp. 90-92.
———, March 2, 1878, pp. 268-69.
———, Sept. 21, 1878, pp. 365-66.
———, Sept. 29, 1883, pp. 400-1.
———, Nov. 21, 1891, p. 590.
———, July 18, 1896, pp. 65-66.
Tablet, April 24, 1858, p. 266.
Westminster Review, CXXII (October, 1884), 559.
Wilde, Oscar, *Pall Mall Gazette*, April 26, 1887. In *Complete Works*, ed. Robert Ross (Boston, 1908), IX, 153-57.
———, *Pall Mall Gazette*, Nov. 24, 1887. In *Works*, IX, 215-20.
———, *Pall Mall Gazette*, Feb. 15, 1889. In *Works*, IX, 425-28.
———, *Pall Mall Gazette*, March 2, 1889. In *Works*, IX, 447-52.

V. LETTERS, MEMOIRS, AND BIOGRAPHIES OF CONTEMPORARIES OF MORRIS

Allingham, William, *William Allingham, a Diary*, ed. H. Allingham and D. Radford (London, 1907).
Blunt, Wilfred Scawen, *My Diaries* (New York, 1922).
Browning, Robert, *Dearest Isa: Robert Browning's Letters to Isabella Blagden*, ed. Edward C. McAleer (Austin, Texas, 1951).
Buckley, Jerome Hamilton, *William Ernest Henley* (Princeton, 1945).
Burne-Jones, Georgiana, *Memorials of Edward Burne-Jones*, 2 vols. (London, 1906).
Carr, J. Comyns, *Some Eminent Victorians* (London, 1908).
Doughty, Oswald, *A Victorian Romantic: Dante Gabriel Rossetti* (London, 1949).
Eliot, George, *The George Eliot Letters*, ed. Gordon S. Haight, 7 vols. (New Haven, 1955).
Gissing, George, *Letters of George Gissing to Members of his Family*, ed. Algernon and Ellen Gissing (Boston, 1927).
Hake, Thomas, and Arthur Compton-Rickett, *The Life and Letters of Theodore Watts-Dunton*, 2 vols. (London, 1916).
Hone, Joseph, *The Life of George Moore* (New York, 1936).
Jacks, Lawrence Pearsall, *Life and Letters of Stopford Brooke*, 2 vols. (London, 1917).
Lafourcade, Georges, *Swinburne* (New York, 1932).
Leon, Derrick, *Ruskin, the Great Victorian* (London, 1949).
Mackail, J. W., and Guy Wyndham, *Life and Letters of George Wyndham*, 2 vols. (London, n. d.).
Meredith, Owen, *Letters from Owen Meredith to Robert and Elizabeth Barrett Browning*, ed. Aurelia and J. Lee Harlan, Jr. (New York, 1936).
———, *Personal and Literary Letters of Robert First Earl of Lytton*, ed. Lady Betty Balfour, 2 vols. (London, 1906).

Patmore, Coventry, *Memoirs and Correspondence of Coventry Patmore*, ed. Basil Champneys, 2 vols. (London, 1900).
Pearson, Hesketh, *Oscar Wilde* (New York, 1946).
Prinsep, Val C., "A Chapter from a Painter's Reminiscence...", *Magazine of Art*, XXVIII (February, 1904), 167-72.
Rossetti, Dante Gabriel, *Dante Gabriel Rossetti, his Family Letters,* ed. with a *Memoir* by W. M. Rossetti, 2 vols. (Boston, 1895).
―――, *Letters of Dante Gabriel Rossetti to William Allingham, 1854-1870*, ed. George Birkbeck Hill (London, 1897).
Rossetti, W. M., ed., *Praeraphaelite Diaries and Letters* (London, 1900).
―――, ed., *Rossetti Papers, 1862 to 1870* (London, 1903).
―――, ed., *Ruskin, Rossetti, Praeraphaelitism* (London, 1899).
Scott, William Bell, *Autobiographical Notes*, ed. W. Minto, 2 vols. (New York, 1892).
Shaw, George Bernard, *William Morris as I Knew Him* (New York, 1936).
Skelton, John, *The Table-Talk of Shirley* (Edinburgh, 1896).
Stevenson, Robert Louis, *The Letters of Robert Louis Stevenson to his Family and Friends*, ed. Sidney Colvin, 2 vols. (London, 1899).
Stringer, Arthur, "William Morris as I Remember Him", *Craftsman*, IV (April, 1903), 126-32.
Swinburne, A. C., *The Swinburne Letters*, ed. Cecil Y. Lang, 6 vols. (New Haven, 1959).
Tennyson, Hallam, *Alfred Lord Tennyson: A Memoir*, 2 vols. (London, 1897).
Terhune, Alfred McKinley, *The Life of Edward Fitzgerald* (New Haven, 1947).
Thorp, Margaret Farrand, *Charles Kingsley* (Princeton, 1937).
White, William Hale, *Letters to Three Friends* (London, 1924).
Yeats, W. B., *Autobiography* (New York, 1938).
―――, "The Happiest of the Poets", *Fortnightly Review*, LXXIX (March 1903), 535-41.
―――, *The Letters of W. B. Yeats*, ed. Allan Wade (New York, 1955).

VI. TWENTIETH-CENTURY CRITICISM

Abrams, M. H., *The Mirror and the Lamp* (New York, 1953).
Altick, Richard D., *The English Common Reader* (Chicago, 1957).
Amis, Kingsley, "Communication and the Victorian Poet", *Essays in Criticism*, IV (October, 1954), 386-99.
Baum, Paull F., *Tennyson Sixty Years After* (Chapel Hill, 1948).
Bevington, Merle Mowbray, *The Saturday Review, 1855-1868* (New York, 1941).
Buckley, Jerome Hamilton, *The Victorian Temper* (Cambridge, Mass., 1951).
Bush, Douglas, *Mythology and the Romantic Tradition in English Poetry* (New York, 1957).
Cruse, Amy, *The Victorians and their Reading* (New York, 1935).
Egan, Rose *The Genesis of the Theory of "Art for Art's Sake" in Germany and in England*, Part II, in *Smith College Studies in Modern Languages*, V (April, 1924), no. 3.
Einarsson, Stefán, "Eirikr Magnússon and his Saga-Translations", *Scandinavian Studies and Notes*, XIII (1934), 17-32.
Eliot, T. S. "Arnold and Pater", *Selected Essays* (New York, 1950), pp. 382-93.

Ellmann, Richard, ed., *Edwardians and Late Victorians* (New York, 1960).
Elton, Oliver, *A Survey of English Literature, 1830-1880*, 2 vols. (London, 1920).
Evans, B. Ifor, *English Poetry in the Later Nineteenth Century* (London, 1933).
―――, "William Morris, his Influence and Reputation", *Contemporary Review*, CXLV (March, 1934), 315-23.
Everett, Edwin Mallard, *The Party of Humanity: The Fortnightly Review and its Contributors, 1865-1874* (Chapel Hill, 1939).
Farley, Frank E., *Scandinavian Influences in the English Romantic Movement*, in *Studies and Notes in Philology and Literature* (Boston, 1903), Volume IX.
Farmer, Albert J., *Le mouvement esthétique et "décadent" en Angleterre* (Paris, 1931).
Foerster, Donald M., *The Fortunes of Epic Poetry* (Catholic University of America Press, 1962).
Ford, George H., *Dickens and his Readers* (Princeton, 1955).
―――, *Keats and the Victorians* (New Haven, 1944).
Graham, Walter, *English Literary Periodicals* (New York, 1930).
Hoare, Dorothy M., *The Works of Morris and Yeats in Relation to Early Saga Literature* (Cambridge, 1937).
Hough, Graham, *The Last Romantics* (London, 1949).
Houghton, Walter E., *The Victorian Frame of Mind, 1830-1870* (New Haven, 1957).
Jackson, Holbrook, *The Eighteen Nineties* (London, 1913).
Jones, William Powell, *Thomas Gray, Scholar* (Cambridge, Mass., 1937).
Jump, J. D., "Weekly Reviewing in the Eighteen-Fifties", *RES*, XXIV (January, 1948), 42-57.
―――, "Weekly Reviewing in the Eighteen-Sixties", *RES*, n. s. III (July, 1952), 244-62.
Litzenberg, Karl, "William Morris and the Reviews", *RES*, XII (1936), 413-28.
Marchand, Leslie, *The Athenaeum* (Chapel Hill, 1941).
Mason, Stuart, *Bibliography of Oscar Wilde* (London, 1914).
Maurer, Oscar, Jr., "William Morris and the Poetry of Escape", *Nineteenth-Century Studies*, ed. Herbert Davis *et al.* (Ithaca, N. Y., 1940), pp. 247-76.
Nordby, Conrad Hjalmar, *The Influence of Old Norse Literature upon English Literature* (New York, 1901).
Richardson, Dorothy, "Saintsbury and Art for Art's Sake in England", *PMLA*, LIX (March, 1944), 243-60.
Roll-Hansen, Diderik, *The Academy, 1869-1879* (Copenhagen, 1957).
Rosenblatt, Louise, *L'Idée de l'art pour l'art dans la Littérature Anglaise pendant la période victorienne* (Paris, 1931).
Shannon, Edgar, Jr., *Tennyson and the Reviewers* (Cambridge, Mass., 1952).
Short, Clarice, "William Morris and Keats", *PMLA*, LIX (1944), 513-23.
Somervell, D. C., "The Reputation of Robert Browning", *Essays and Studies*, XV (1929), 122-39.
Thomas, William Beach, *The Story of the Spectator, 1828-1928* (London, 1928).
Tillotson, Geoffrey, *Criticism and the Nineteenth Century* (London, 1951).
Tinker, C. B., and H. F. Lowry, *The Poetry of Matthew Arnold* (London, 1940).
Warren, Alba H., Jr., *English Poetic Theory, 1825-1865* (Princeton, 1950).

West, Paul, "A Note on the 1890's", *English*, XII (Spring, 1958), 54-57.
Williams, Raymond, *Culture and Society, 1780-1950* (London, 1959).
Wolff, Michael, "The Rubáiyát's Neglected Reviewer", *Victorian Newsletter*, no. 17 (Spring, 1960), pp. 4-6.

INDEX

Abrams, M. H., 117
Aesthetes, 4, 5, 6, 11, 12, 13, 14, 31, 108
Alford, Henry, 40
Amis, Kingsley, 124
Arnold, Matthew, 11, 12, 20, 21, 68, 70, 121

Bailey, Philip James, 1, 2
Baldwin, Mrs. Alfred, 84
Baudelaire, Charles, 9
Baum, Paull, 3
Bax, Belfort, 90
Bayne, Thomas, 30, 42, 55, 66, 74
Blackwood, John, 42
Blagden, Isabella, 56
Blake, William, 10
"Bloody Sunday", 87
Blunt, Wilfred Scawen, 86, 117
Browning, Robert, 2, 3, 7, 17, 19, 20, 25, 28, 38, 52, 56, 120
Buchanan, Robert, 41
Buckley, Jerome, 5
Burden, Jane, 35
Burne-Jones, Edward, 6, 8, 17, 21, 25, 32, 82, 98
Burne-Jones, Georgiana, 88, 89
Bush, Douglas, 120
Byron, George Lord, 1, 99

Calverly, C. S., 26
Carlyle, Thomas, 67, 85
Carr, J. Comyns, 120
Chants for Socialists, 53, 89, 94, 95
Chaucer, Geoffrey, 8, 35, 36, 37, 38, 43, 44, 45, 48, 49, 50, 51, 52, 53, 54, 55, 120
Chorley, Henry, 19, 26
Coleridge, S. T., 99
Colvin, Sidney, 39, 63, 65
Courthope, W. J., 43
Cruse, Amy, 22

Dasent, Sir George Webbe, 67, 68
Defence of Guenevere, The 8, 17-32, 69, 92, 100, 115, 118, 119, 120, 123, 124
Democratic Federation, 86, 99
Dixon, R. W., 17, 20

Doughty, Oswald, 19
Dowden, Edward, 53
Dowson, Ernest, 12
Dream of John Ball, A, 89, 90, 92, 96, 103, 105, 106, 107, 112, 113
Dufferin, Lord, 67

Earthly Paradise, The, 9, 18, 35-57 69, 83, 90, 91, 92, 93, 98, 99, 100, 115, 116, 117, 118 119, 120, 121, 123, 124, 125
Eastern Question Association, 84
Egan, Rose, 4
Eliot, George, 42
Ellis, F. S., 117, 118, 122, 123
Elton Charles, 112
Evans, B. Ifor, 68

Farley, Frank, 67
Farmer, Albert J., 5
Fitzgerald, Edward, 38
Foerster, Donald M., 117
Ford, George, 6, 7, 54, 81
Forman, Harry Buxton, 44, 45, 46, 49, 54, 61, 65, 66, 71, 89, 93, 108
Fraser, George, 63, 64
Froissart, Jean, 17
Fulford, William, 17

Gissing, George, 98
Glasier, Bruce, 87
Gosse, Edmund, 71, 73, 74, 76
Gray, Thomas, 67, 68
Grennan, Margaret, 82

Hallam, Arthur, 1, 2, 3
Hammersmith Socialist Society, 86, 90
Head, Sir Edmund, 68
Henderson, Fred, 122
Henley, W. E., 5
Herbert, William, 67
Hewlett, Henry G., 27, 62, 63, 71, 75, 111
Hewlett, Maurice, 100
Horne, R. H., 2
Hotten, John, 10
Hough, Graham, 36
Houghton, Walter, 116

House of the Wolfings, The, 90, 103, 104, 108, 109, 110, 111, 112, 113, 122
Hunt, Holman, 6, 8, 18
Hyndman, Henry, 86

Jackson, Holbrook, 5
Johnson, Lionel, 12
Jump, J. D., 21

Keats, John, 2, 3, 6, 8, 17, 36, 54, 81
Kelmscott Press, 18, 90, 122
Kipling, Rudyard, 5
Knight, Joseph, 20, 22, 23, 27, 28, 29

Laing, Samuel, 67
Lang, Andrew, 25, 29, 31, 46, 47, 51, 65
Lewes, G. H., 42
Life and Death of Jason, The, 18, 35-57, 69, 100, 115, 116, 118, 119, 120, 123, 124
Litzenberg, Karl, 119
Love Is Enough, 59-66, 69, 100, 116, 119, 120, 121, 122, 123, 124, 125

MacDonell, Annie, 28, 38, 51
Mackail, J. W., 8, 18, 35, 59, 60, 69, 117, 119, 120
Magnüssen, Eirikr, 59, 67, 68
Mallet, Paul Henri, 67, 68
Malory, Sir Thomas, 17
Maurer, Oscar Jr. 56
Meredith, George, 9, 66
Meredith, Owen, 25
Millais, John Everett, 6, 18
Milton, John, 43
Morley, Henry, 71
Morley, John, 10, 13, 39
Morris, Jenny, 35
Morris, May, 35, 48, 60, 66, 87, 118, 119
Morshead, E. D. A., 70

News from Nowhere, 89, 92, 96, 100, 103, 105, 106, 107, 112, 113

Oxford Brotherhood, 9, 17, 25, 117

Parker, John, 24
Pater, Walter, 4, 9, 11, 12, 13, 14, 28, 46, 51, 54
Patmore, Coventry, 19, 22, 65
Payne, J. B., 10
Percy, Thomas, 67
Pilgrims of Hope, 89, 93, 94, 95
Poems by the Way, 90, 91, 92, 93, 95
Powell, George E. J., 68
Pre-Raphaelites, 5, 6, 8, 9, 17-32, 108, 119
Price, Cormel, 17, 81, 124
Prinsep, Valentine, 17, 25

Quiller-Couch, Arthur, 40

Richardson, Dorothy, 4
Romantic Movement, 1
Roots of the Mountains, The, 103, 104, 108, 109, 111, 112
Rosenblatt, Louise, 4, 9, 115
Rossetti, D. G., 4, 6, 7, 8, 9, 11, 13, 14, 17, 18, 20, 21, 22, 24, 28, 29, 32, 38, 39, 41, 56, 60, 82, 108, 120
Rossetti, W. M., 7, 19, 25
Ruskin, John, 8, 19, 23, 25, 70, 82, 85

Saintsbury, George, 25, 27, 28, 29, 31, 43, 51, 56, 92, 108, 109, 111
Scheu, Andreas, 86
Scott, Sir Walter, 67, 68
Scott, William Bell, 25, 60
Sharp, Amy, 30, 31, 55
Shaw, George Bernard, 5, 87, 96, 97
Shelley, Percy, 1, 8, 81, 82, 99
Shorter, Clement, 83
Signs of Change, 89, 92
Simcox, G. A., 51, 63, 64, 77
Skelton, John, 18, 22, 24, 29, 44, 47, 49
Smith, Nowell, 72
Social Democratic Federation, 86, 89

INDEX

Socialism, its Growth and Outcome, 90, 92
Socialist League, 86, 87, 89
Society for the Protection of Ancient Buildings, 85, 122
Somervell, D. C., 3
Southey, Robert, 99
Spencer, Edmund, 8, 54
Statham, H. H., 30, 77
Steele, Robert, 113
Story of Sigurd the Volsung, The, 59, 66-78, 81, 90, 99, 100, 104, 116, 117, 120, 121, 122, 123
Story of the Glittering Plain, The, 103, 104, 108, 111, 112, 113
Sundering Flood, The, 103, 108
Swinburne, A. C., 4, 6, 8, 9, 10, 11, 12, 13, 14, 21, 24, 27, 39, 41, 45, 48, 55, 70, 88, 89, 99, 107, 108
Symons, Arthur, 4, 5, 50, 65, 78, 108, 109, 110, 111, 116

Taylor, Henry, 1, 8
Temple, Ruth, 12
Tennyson, Alfred Lord, 1, 2, 3, 8, 17, 19, 20, 24, 27, 52, 98
Thompson, E. P., 95
Thorpe, Benjamin, 68
Tillotson, Geoffrey, 12
Traill, H. D., 97, 98
Tupper, Martin, 2
Tynan, Katharine, 96

Vallance, Aymer, 54
VanDyke, Henry, 2
Vaughan, C. E., 61

Warren, Alba, 4, 78
Water of the Wondrous Isles, The, 103, 106, 108, 109, 110, 122,
Watts-Dunton, Theodore, 70, 71, 73, 76, 96, 107, 108, 109, 117, 121
Webb, Philip, 122
Well at the World's End, The, 103, 106, 108
Wells, H. G., 5

Wilde, Oscar, 4, 5, 6, 9, 11, 12, 40, 41, 95, 96, 108, 109, 110, 111
Wood Beyond the World, The, 103, 105, 108, 110, 112, 118
Wordsworth, William, 43
Wyndham, George, 5

Yeats, W. B., 4, 5, 9, 11, 13, 96, 108, 112, 122